ANNUAL UPDATE **2017**

UK GOVERNMENT & POLITICS

Neil McNaughton
Eric Magee

ODDER
UCATION
HACHETTE UK COMPANY

Hodder Education, an Hachette UK company, Blenheim Court, George Street, Banbury, Oxfordshire OX16 5BH

Orders
Bookpoint Ltd, 130 Park Drive, Milton Park, Abingdon, Oxfordshire OX14 4SE
tel: 01235 827827
fax: 01235 400401
e-mail: education@bookpoint.co.uk

Lines are open 9.00 a.m.–5.00 p.m., Monday to Saturday, with a 24-hour message answering service. You can also order through the Hodder Education website: www.hoddereducation.co.uk

ISBN 978-1-4718-6799-6

First printed 2017

Impression number 5 4 3 2 1
Year 2020 2019 2018 2017

Typeset by Integra Software Services Pvt. Ltd., Pondicherry, India

Cover photo: Kevin Smart/iStock

Printed by CPI Group (UK) Ltd, Croydon, CR0 4YY

Hachette UK's policy is to use papers that are natural, renewable and recyclable products and made from wood grown in sustainable forests. The logging and manufacturing processes are expected to conform to the environmental regulations of the country of origin.

Contents

Contents

Chapter 1

The EU referendum: why did 'Leave' win?

Exam success

The up-to-date facts, examples and arguments in this chapter will help you to produce good-quality answers in your AS unit tests in the following areas of the specifications.

Edexcel	AQA	OCR
Unit 1 Democracy and political participation	**Unit 1** Participation	**Unit F851** Participation and voting

Context

It was a considerable surprise when the UK voted to leave the European Union on 23 June 2016. Even Nigel Farage, the most prominent 'Leave' campaigner, was not convinced that his side could win. The opinion polls did predict a close result, but for most of the run-up to the vote they were showing a comfortable 'Remain' lead. Senior politicians were confused too. Several of them, the prime minister and chancellor of the exchequer included, pinned their careers on a 'Stay' vote. They were both to lose their jobs.

The question we have to ask, therefore, is how did this come about when so many were predicting the opposite? In Chapter 2 we examine the question of how democratic the exercise has been; this chapter will examine why the result was as it was. A word of caution is needed. The conclusions described here have to be provisional. It can take years to conclude research on the reasons behind voting in elections and referendums, so we will not know all the answers for some time. However, both research already undertaken and the opinions of knowledgeable commentators can tell us a great deal now.

Economic factors

In the campaign many organisations warned that, if the UK were to leave the EU, there would be dire economic consequences. The UK Treasury, the Bank of England, the International Monetary Fund (IMF) and the Organisation for Economic Cooperation and Development (OECD) all predicted recession and a decline in the UK's economic fortunes. Yet, despite being bombarded with such warnings, the electorate was unmoved. Two factors may have been at work here:

■ There is general disillusionment with senior politicians and experts in the country. Put simply, they are not believed, especially after they failed to head off the economic crisis and recession after 2008.

■ Although these economic organisations stressed the economic benefits of EU membership, in many parts of the country, notably the northeast and northwest, parts of the West Country, and parts of Wales and Scotland, these benefits were not apparent. Persistent economic stagnation, the decline of traditional industries and long-term unemployment are characteristics of such areas. To plagiarise a famous line from the Monty Python film, *Life of Brian*, the people asked, 'What did the European Union ever do for us?' The answer appeared to be 'Very little'. There did not seem very much to lose by leaving.

Immigration

One of the interesting findings of the regional variation in voting is that there was often a strong Leave vote in areas where there were relatively few European migrants, for example in the West Country and Wales, while in areas of high immigration, notably the big cities, there were Stay majorities. It is, therefore, largely *fear of* immigration that is at work here. Among these fears, Turkey played a huge part. Though the government insisted that Turkey would not be joining the EU for the foreseeable future, many voters believed Nigel Farage's exhortation that we were about to open a huge portal in the east which would allow many millions of migrants to pour into western Europe, including the UK.

Some communities which have experienced large-scale immigration, largely of migrant agricultural workers, did vote Leave — not for economic reasons, but because they felt their communities were being overrun by foreigners. This occurred in Lincolnshire, East Anglia, Essex and parts of Kent.

Personalities

There is little doubt that some of the Leave campaigners caught the imagination of voters, much more than the 'conventional' politicians who were mostly for Remain. Boris Johnson and Nigel Farage, in particular, were not seen as members of the 'old guard' that had let Britain down in the past. Farage was a complete outsider and Johnson, though a Conservative, was seen as something of a maverick. They were viewed as fresh and more honest than other politicians. By contrast, David Cameron and Jeremy Corbyn had low personal popularity ratings and were less trusted.

The Labour Party

The Labour Party found it difficult to campaign for Remain for a number of reasons. First, it was deeply divided over the leadership of Jeremy Corbyn and so was in a state of disarray. Secondly, the left wing of the party was gaining influence and the left has traditionally been opposed to the European ideal. Many on the left see the European Union as a kind of 'capitalist club', whose policies of free trade and free labour markets are designed to help large-scale capitalist enterprises *against* the interests of both workers and consumers — a belief that is common, even though one of the founders of the European Community in the 1950s, Jean Monnet, was himself a socialist.

Though it was official Labour policy to remain in the EU, there was a lack of enthusiasm in the party's campaigning and a suspicion that Corbyn himself was not convinced of the case for remaining in. Most trade unions were relatively silent on the issue and so it was UKIP that was making the running in many of the UK's industrialised areas.

Age

The older generation tends to vote in much larger numbers than the young (see Chapter 2). It is also true that the elderly were much more inclined to want to leave the EU than the young. There was therefore a natural bias in the voting towards Leave. Table 2.4 in Chapter 2 shows that the early research suggests that only 27% of the 18–24 age group voted to leave, while 60% of the over-65s voted to leave.

There is logic in this outcome as the elderly have much less of a stake in EU membership than the young, who will be affected for a long time into the future.

Return of the non-voters

The polling organisation Number Cruncher Politics (**www.ncpolitics.uk**) has analysed voting in the referendum and concludes that possibly as many as two million people who do not normally vote, *did* vote in the referendum, partly explaining the relatively high turnout of 72%. Furthermore, as many of these were disillusioned non-voters, largely blue-collar workers and unemployed, many of them voted for Leave as this was a chance for their voices to be heard and they knew that every vote would count.

A deeper malaise

It is an interesting footnote that Donald Trump tweeted in August 2016, at the height of his presidential campaign, 'They will soon be calling me Mr Brexit'. It was a typically flippant Trump remark, but it carried a deeper significance. The Trump message to Americans was similar to the messages being transmitted in the referendum campaign. This can be viewed in two senses.

Nativism

The term 'nativism' refers to a political and cultural attitude that suggests the indigenous, established population of a country should have a higher status than other people who have entered a country later. In its extreme form this can amount to racism, but in a more moderate form it is simply discriminatory against certain people. Donald Trump is a self-confessed nativist of the latter kind. He believes the 'American people' should 'come first' and have their interests protected against immigrants, legal and illegal, and that the American economy should be protected from outside competition to protect 'American jobs'.

UKIP has also tapped into such nativist sentiment in Britain. Some of its campaign to leave the EU was about 'British jobs for British workers' (ironically, an expression used by Labour prime minister Gordon Brown nine years before) and about protecting British culture against an onslaught from competing foreign ways of life, arriving from and through the European mainland.

When the result of the referendum was announced, Nigel Farage declared that this was 'Independence Day'. It was a significant remark. It demonstrated that part of the Leave message was that the UK would be able to regain its sovereignty, a powerful attraction for those who fear that the UK has been losing its distinctive identity.

Populism

This is a movement very much on the march in Europe and the USA. It can be both right wing, as in the case of Donald Trump in the USA, the National Front in France, the Party for Freedom in the Netherlands and UKIP in Britain, and left wing, as in the case of Bernie Sanders in the USA, Podemos in Spain and SYRIZA in Greece. Populism blames many modern ills on vested interests that act against the interests of individuals and small enterprises. Populists attack big government generally, large multinational corporations, the financial establishment and international organisations that threaten national sovereignty. The European Union is one such international organisation.

In the UK it is largely, though not exclusively, the white working class that supports populism, of both the right and the left. This is why UKIP and the Labour Party find themselves in competition for the support of the same groups. They have different ideas about how to combat the forces that damage the interests of the poorer working class, but they share the same critique of contemporary economic and political structures.

So the Leave campaign was bolstered by the wider, right-wing populist movement. The European Union was viewed as just one of the causes (through neglect) of economic stagnation and lack of opportunity in some regions, along with Westminster politicians, large corporations and the banking system.

The general conclusion arising from the growth of nativism and populism is that it was the votes of those who saw the appeal of Nigel Farage's message that tipped the balance over to the Leave verdict. In other words, many of those who voted to leave were not specifically disillusioned with the European Union, but were voting against the traditional political and economic forces that were holding them back. Many such disillusioned people complained that nobody in the political establishment listened to them. Indeed, many had even given up voting altogether until June 2016. Then, along came a chance to punish the establishment, to make their voices heard for once.

Conclusion

The reasons why the UK voted to leave the European Union are extremely complex. No single reason can be identified as the key factor. There were several forces at work. To summarise, these included the following:

- The Leave campaign proved to be more influential than the Remain campaign. This was especially true of economic issues. The Leave leaders also proved to be more charismatic than the Remain campaigners.
- Immigration was a huge factor. A number of news items giving negative images of migrants in the UK and in Calais, waiting to enter the UK, were especially important to a country already nervous about the scale of immigration in recent years.
- As usual, older people voted in larger numbers than the young. Older people, who tend to be more conservative, are more likely to see the European Union as a 'socialist' experiment and a threat to national sovereignty.
- A sizeable cohort of normally non-voters decided to take the opportunity to vote and express their dissatisfaction with the political establishment.
- The Leave vote was part of a wider populist, nativist movement which is taking hold among blue-collar workers and the long-term unemployed.

Exam focus

To consolidate your knowledge of this chapter, answer the following questions:

1 What is meant by the term 'populism'?
2 What is meant by the term 'nativism'?
3 Why have left-wing politicians often opposed the European Union?
4 In what senses can opposition to the European Union be seen as 'right wing'?
5 Why is immigration seen as a problem in the UK?

Chapter 2

Referendums: a triumph for popular democracy or a flawed democratic process?

Exam success

The up-to-date facts, examples and arguments in this chapter will help you to produce good-quality answers in your AS unit tests in the following areas of the specifications.

Edexcel	AQA	OCR
Unit 1	**Unit 1**	**Unit F851**
Democracy and political participation	Participation	Participation and voting

Context

This chapter mainly considers the referendum on UK membership of the European Union which took place on 23 June 2016, but it also looks back at the 2014 referendum on Scottish independence and the 2011 poll on reform of the electoral system. Comparisons between these three referendums can tell us a good deal about the democratic credentials of referendums in general.

In order to evaluate referendums, it is necessary to look at the generally agreed advantages and disadvantages of this important democratic device, a device which appears to be becoming increasingly popular in recent times as a way of settling key political and constitutional issues. We can use this assessment as a guide to how democratically successful these three recent votes were. Table 2.1 summarises the main arguments on both sides of the issue.

Table 2.1 The advantages and disadvantages of referendums

Advantages	Disadvantages
1 They are a pure form of democracy, the voice of the people and the verdict of the majority.	4 It is often said that they represent the 'tyranny of the majority'. The minority, which is outvoted, may feel itself oppressed by the majority.
2 They can settle conflicts that threaten to divide either the political system or the nation generally, or both. They can be a unifying force.	5 They reduce issues to a 'binary' yes/no question when often they are more complex than that.
3 When decisions involve generational changes, often to the constitution and the way people are governed, referendums can entrench them, preventing them being overturned by a future government and parliament.	6 Some issues may be too complex and difficult for the majority of people to understand fully. Many may be voting out of ignorance.
	7 Voters may be easily persuaded by charismatic, populist leaders and by tabloid media that appeal to their emotions rather than their reason.
	8 It can happen that the voters are actually delivering a verdict on a different issue. In particular, a referendum might be used to express dissatisfaction with the performance of the government rather than a view on the issue itself.

An assessment of the 2016 EU referendum

We can now examine the EU referendum on the basis of these positive and negative criteria.

1 A pure form of democracy?

The EU referendum was arguably the most important democratic exercise that the UK has ever undertaken, more important than any past referendum or any general election. Political and constitutional changes normally occur slowly. This was a momentous event, a throwback to the very origins of direct democracy in ancient Athens when the people gathered to decide on such issues as war or peace and how the city was to be governed. It was made clear before the vote that the verdict of the people would stick. There was to be no second consideration of the question for at least a generation.

In addition, the turnout of 72.2% was encouraging. This was a genuine test of public opinion. However, given the majority of 52% to leave, this means that only 37.5% of the adult population actually voted to leave.

2 A unifying force?

Here there was a major problem. Far from unifying the UK, this vote created a huge divide. Perhaps more accurately, the nation was already divided over membership of the EU and related issues, and the referendum simply laid bare this fault line. Even the newspaper headlines reflected this:

Brexit Earthquake (*Times*)
Over and Out (*Guardian*)
So What the Hell Happens Now? (*Daily Mirror*)
Disunited Kingdom (*Scottish Daily Mail*)

The biggest problem was the fact that the voters of Scotland voted decisively for the UK to stay in the EU. This indicated a fundamental division between Scotland and England. Table 2.2 indicates the difference between the voting in different parts of the UK.

Table 2.2 Voting by national region

Country	% who voted to leave the EU
England	53
Scotland	38
Wales	53
Northern Ireland	44

The Northern Ireland vote reveals a division in that society which is complicated by the fact that there has been an open border between the province and the Republic of Ireland which will become closed when the UK leaves the EU. That aside, the vote threatens to cause further problems in an already divided society. The Republicans will argue that the interests of Northern Ireland will be damaged by Brexit (the province has received a great deal of EU aid) and that this is another example of British domination of the Irish.

The shockwave was even more powerful in Scotland, with renewed demands for a second referendum on independence. The Scots felt they were being pulled out of the EU against their will.

It also demonstrated a class divide in the UK, as shown in Table 2.3. We can see a stark difference between the attitude of the working class and the wealthier middle classes.

Table 2.3 Class and voting in the EU referendum

Social class group	% who voted to leave the EU
AB	43
C1	51
C2	64
DE	64

AB = best off; C1 = better-off middle class; C2 = less well-off middle class;
DE = poorer working class.

Sources: *The Times* newspaper and Ashcroft poll, 25 June 2016

UK Government & Politics

A similar divide can be seen in different age groups (see Table 2.4). Put simply, the older the voter, the more likely they were to vote to leave the EU. Turnout among older votes was much higher than among the young, so the age effect was exaggerated. This creates a problem in that, arguably, the generation that has the biggest stake in the future of the UK was outvoted by a generation which has, by definition, less of a stake.

Table 2.4 Age and voting in the EU referendum

Age group	% who voted to leave the EU
18–24	27
25–34	38
35–44	48
45–54	56
55–64	57
65+	60

Sources: *The Times* newspaper and Ashcroft poll, 25 June 2016

Voting in England was very even between the different regions, with one notable exception. In London only 40% of voters opted to leave the EU, compared to the English regions where leave voting varied between 55 and 59%.

In summary, therefore, schisms were revealed between:
- the young and the old
- England and Scotland
- London and the rest of England
- the well-off and the poor

The outcome also caused the government itself to fall apart. The prime minister fell from power along with nearly half the cabinet. It was left to unenthusiastic 'Remain' campaigner, Theresa May, to try to re-unite the government. The Labour Party also fell apart, with the moderate, pro-Remain wing blaming Jeremy Corbyn's poor campaign for the Brexit vote. It seemed that the masonry of the political system had been shaken to the point of collapse.

Possibly more seriously than all the above, the campaign and result suggested a deep division between people and the political system itself. Many of those who voted to leave apparently did so as a protest against a political establishment that simply does not listen to their concerns. This referendum was their one and only chance to express their dissatisfaction.

3 Has it entrenched the decision to leave?

There were immediate calls to revisit the issue after the vote, but the new prime minister, Theresa May, insisted that 'Brexit means Brexit' and that the UK will be leaving the EU. Although 4.2 million people signed an e-petition asking for a

second referendum, this was immediately rejected. The argument was presented that the British people had been 'duped' during the campaign.

The decision is also irrevocable. It seems highly unlikely that the UK will be allowed to re-apply for membership and even less likely that the EU would allow the UK back in.

4 Does it represent the 'tyranny of the majority'?

Certainly the Scots and the young will say yes, as will much of the population of London. We may also ask whether a majority of 52–48% is decisive enough for such a momentous choice. Furthermore, the fact that only 37.5% of the adult population actually voted to leave is, in reality, the 'tyranny of the *minority*'.

In democratic terms there is a real problem concerning Scotland. Unionist supporters say that the UK is one single community, so the various parts must accept the verdict of the majority. Scottish nationalists, on the other hand, suggest that Scotland is a separate community being dragged out of the EU against its will.

However, there will always be a losing minority after a referendum; that is the reality of direct democracy. It will be a stern test of the unity of the United Kingdom whether that minority can accept the rule of the majority.

5 Was it really a binary decision?

On the face of it, it certainly was — to leave or not to leave, yes or no. However, it could be argued that a more subtle outcome could have been reached. This would have been a changed relationship with the EU but not a complete divorce. Indeed, the outgoing prime minister, David Cameron, had attempted to negotiate such a changed relationship in the run-up to the referendum campaign.

It soon became clear that Cameron had failed to achieve any meaningful reforms, notably over the problem of the free movement of labour. It is an interesting question what the outcome of the vote would have been, had he been able to obtain agreement on significant curbs on immigration and reductions in the UK's financial contributions to the EU budget.

Opponents of holding a referendum argued that it would have been possible to change the UK's relationship with the EU sufficiently to satisfy public opinion. In other words, it need not have been a binary decision; there could have been a nuanced, more subtle change.

6 Was the issue too complex for the average voter?

In some ways the issue of EU membership was extremely complex, not least because nobody could truly predict what would happen if the UK were to leave the EU. The economic consequences of either remaining or leaving were, indeed, so complicated that even experts could not agree. This left the electorate somewhat bewildered. It was also unclear what the scale of the UK's financial contribution to the EU budget actually was.

On the other hand, two of the key issues — immigration and the fact that the UK has lost a good deal of sovereignty to the EU — proved to be more visceral, or emotional, than rational. Many of those who voted to leave did so because they were concerned by the effects of large-scale migration from Europe on British society and on domestic jobs. Similarly, many voters were simply disillusioned with the amount of interference in domestic affairs being wielded by the European Union and its so-called 'undemocratic' institutions. The term 'Brussels bureaucrats' was often used in the campaign. These two issues could certainly be widely understood.

7 Were the voters swayed by emotional appeals by populist leaders and the tabloids?

Two key figures came into play here. They were Nigel Farage, long-time UKIP anti-EU campaigner, and former London mayor, Boris Johnson. Johnson declared his hand late in the day, but his intervention was decisive. Both had a considerable following among the general public. They were seen as 'outside the political establishment' and therefore more trustworthy. In contrast, the established political leaders, such as David Cameron and Jeremy Corbyn, failed to capture the public imagination. It is interesting that the Scottish first minister, Nicola Sturgeon, possibly Britain's most popular politician, *did* manage to persuade a large majority of her countrymen and women to support the Remain side. So individuals did make a difference.

The majority of the press recommended a Leave vote. Table 2.5 indicates which way the main newspapers suggested their readers should vote. At first sight this looks quite balanced, but it should be noted that the two main high-volume tabloids, the *Sun* and the *Mail*, both backed Leave.

Table 2.5 What did the newspapers recommend?

Newspaper	Recommendation
Daily Mail	Leave
Sun	Leave
Daily Mirror	Remain
Daily Telegraph	Leave
The Times	Remain
Guardian	Remain
Daily Express	Leave
Independent	Remain

Some of the headlines also carried a highly emotional appeal to the voters. On the whole, they were appeals to patriotism, suggesting the whole future of Britain was at stake. For example:

New EU Threat to your Pension (*Daily Express*)

BeLEAVE in Britain (*Sun*)

If you believe in Britain vote Leave (*Daily Mail*)

The pro-Leave tabloids also ran a relentless stream of stories pointing out the negative aspects of immigration. This contrasted with the more measured, rational approach of the broadsheets, which on the whole were more pro-EU.

8 Were the voters *really* voting on the issue of the EU?

Clearly many were, but there has also been some concern that much of the Leave vote was actually a vote against the 'Westminster bubble', against politicians who do not listen to, or understand, the concerns of those who have been left behind by globalisation and growing inequality. Much research still needs to be done, but it appears that many people who normally see voting as futile, did seize this chance to express their deep dissatisfaction.

In this sense the referendum was and was not democratic. It *did* give a voice to those who felt neglected; it was a chance for many to defy the established politicians and exercise their popular will. But, if many voted on a completely different issue, it could be said that the outcome of the referendum was a false one and that generations to come will have to live with it.

A final, possibly rather one-sided, verdict on the EU referendum was handed down by the Electoral Reform Society in the September after the poll. Its report, *It's Good To Talk: Doing Referendums Differently after the EU Vote* (September 2016) made the following criticisms:

- The campaign was too short to debate the issues thoroughly enough.
- Most voters felt ill-informed by the time they voted. The Society's research suggested that only 33% of voters felt 'well informed'.
- Too much of the campaigning was negative. Both sides, but especially the Remain camp, failed to concentrate on the positive side of their case.
- The Leave campaign in particular made false or misleading claims.

The Electoral Reform Society recommends, therefore, stricter rules in future on how referendums are conducted. Its report suggested that democracy had not been well served in this campaign. Interestingly, the same report praised the campaign on Scottish independence as being more thorough, open and honest.

A comparison with the Scottish independence referendum, 2014

In comparison with the EU referendum, we can summarise both the positive and negative aspects of the Scottish poll.

Positives

- The result, at 55–45%, was decisive enough, especially with a high turnout of 84.6%.
- The results were much more evenly spread in terms of age, social class and region. This meant that there were no major minorities who felt discriminated against by the referendum result.
- It brought large numbers of younger people into the political process, including voters aged 16 and 17. The EU referendum saw a much lower turnout among the younger age groups. In the EU referendum, it is estimated that only 36%

of 18–24-year-olds voted (a figure still to be verified), whereas in the Scottish referendum, 75% of 16–17-year-olds and 54% of 18–24-year-olds voted.

- In the end it was not just a binary vote. We saw that the EU referendum had a simple Leave or Remain answer. At first sight this is also true of the Scottish vote. However, in the aftermath of the Scottish referendum, Westminster politicians agreed to grant much wider powers, including over tax and welfare, to the Scottish government. So the Scots voted against independence, but did achieve a compromise of more autonomous powers for their government. It seems less likely that such an outcome will occur over the EU.
- The Electoral Reform Society reported that the Scottish referendum was conducted in a more open and honest way, with more rational arguments.

Negatives
- It was a rather one-sided campaign in that the 'No to Independence' side was acknowledged to have run an ineffective, negative campaign. Had they been more effective, it has been suggested that the No vote would have been more decisive.
- Like the EU referendum, it did expose how divided the Scottish people are over the issue of independence.
- It did not settle the issue, especially after the UK's decision to leave the EU. With most Scots being pro-EU, the demand for independence has been rekindled.

A comparison with the 2011 referendum on the introduction of AV for general elections in the UK

The 2011 referendum on whether the UK should adopt the Alternative Vote (AV) system for general elections in place of the first-past-the-post system was called by the coalition government. The Liberal Democrat party leadership insisted on the vote as part of its agreement to cooperate with the Conservative Party. The result was a very decisive No by 67.9–32.1% on a low turnout of 42.2%. It was very different from the Scottish and EU referendums.

Positives
- The result was decisive and the issue was settled.
- It did not divide the country, as the No vote was widespread.
- The debate was relatively balanced and rational.

Negatives
- The system chosen for reform — AV — was rather complex and many people complained that they did not fully understand it.
- Similarly, people found it difficult to comprehend the *consequences* of change.
- The outcome discriminated against small political parties that had an interest in reform but were not wealthy or influential enough to campaign on a level playing field.
- It was argued that the referendum was held in order to prevent a schism within the ruling coalition rather than in the interests of better democracy.

■ The Liberal Democrat Party itself was very unpopular at the time. It was blamed for breaking its promise to oppose the introduction of higher university tuition fees. Many voters, therefore, used the referendum to punish the Liberal Democrats. Opinion polls suggested there was a majority of support for reform, just not *this* kind of reform and not one supported by Liberal Democrats.

It could never be argued that the vote on electoral reform was remotely as important as the vote on EU membership, so a comparison is difficult. On the other hand, the referendum on Scottish independence was comparable — at least as far as the Scots are concerned. Nevertheless, if we put the three together, we can find illustrations of *all* the positive and negative aspects of the use of referendums.

Conclusion

Was the EU referendum a democratic triumph or was it a flawed exercise? We can say it was successful in these senses:

■ The turnout was high, so most of the politically aware population participated.
■ It settled an issue that threatened to divide the political system and the nation for a generation.
■ It transcended the political community, which has come into considerable disrepute in recent years.

But it was also flawed in these ways:

■ The result was close and had the effect of dividing rather than uniting the nation.
■ Many of the losing side claimed that the result was distorted as a result of too many dishonest claims made by the winning side.
■ Many argued — including many of the voters themselves — that this issue was too complex for many people to understand.
■ It had the effect of destabilising Scotland, many of whose inhabitants felt they were being forced into a decision they opposed by the English.

It may be that only time will tell us whether this referendum was a success or a terrible mistake.

Exam focus

To consolidate your knowledge of this chapter, answer the following questions:

1 Why are referendums sometimes described as the 'tyranny of the majority'?
2 Why are some issues the subject of a referendum?
3 What are the main ways in which referendums can be flawed?
4 Should the issue of UK membership of the EU have been settled by government and Parliament rather than by the people?
5 Did the 2016 EU referendum divide or unite the nation?

Chapter 3

Theresa May: how and why did she become prime minister?

Context

On 24 June 2016, David Cameron appeared outside 10 Downing Street and announced his intention to resign both as prime minister and as leader of the Conservative Party. His resignation was to take effect as soon as the Conservative Party had elected a new leader. This process was expected to take until the autumn. However, by 12 July Theresa May had been declared the new Tory leader and so she took over from Cameron much earlier than expected. How had this occurred? Why was it so fast? What is its likely significance and what kind of prime minister is Mrs May going to be? This chapter seeks to answer these questions.

Cameron resigned because the referendum on UK membership of the EU had produced an unexpected 'Leave' decision. Not only had Cameron been defeated, making his position as head of government untenable, but also he did not feel he could lead the country out of the EU when he had campaigned to stay in. An immediate irony emerged from this as Theresa May herself had declared in favour of remaining in the EU. Two realities differentiated her from Cameron: first, she had never been an especially enthusiastic supporter of EU membership (she scarcely spoke or appeared in the campaign); and secondly, she was not head of government and therefore not head of the 'Remain' side, so she had not been personally defeated. How she captured the leadership of her party is a more complex story.

The Conservative Party leadership process

The election of a new Conservative leader occurs in four stages:

- **Stage 1.** Nominations go before Conservative MPs and a ballot is held. The candidate coming bottom of this poll withdraws and a second ballot takes place.
- **Stage 2.** A second ballot is held and again the candidate finishing last must withdraw.
- **Stage 3.** More ballots occur until only two candidates remain.
- **Stage 4.** The two remaining candidates are offered to the wider membership of the party, who vote for one or the other. The winner is elected leader.

The purpose of this system is to ensure that a leader is found who is acceptable to *both* the wider party membership *and* the MPs in Parliament. This contrasts starkly with the Labour situation in the summer of 2016, where one candidate for the leadership — the incumbent Jeremy Corbyn — was very popular with the wider party membership but was unacceptable to most Labour MPs, while his opponent, Owen Smith, was in the opposite position.

In the event, the Conservative election was curtailed. In the first ballot, the votes by MPs were as follows:

Table 3.1 Results of the first ballot

Candidate	Votes
Theresa May (Home Secretary)	165
Andrea Leadsom (Minister for Climate Change and Energy)	66
Michael Gove (Justice Secretary)	48
Stephen Crabb (Work and Pensions Secretary)	34
Liam Fox (Former Defence Secretary)	16

Liam Fox was eliminated and Stephen Crabb withdrew voluntarily.

Table 3.2 Results of the second ballot

Candidate	Votes
Theresa May	199
Andrea Leadsom	84
Michael Gove	46

Michael Gove was eliminated but Andrea Leadsom also withdrew voluntarily. This meant that Theresa May was elected unopposed.

The implications of this were threefold:

1 There is no doubt that there was a very large consensus of support for Mrs May in the parliamentary party.

2 Theresa May was not elected by the wider party membership, so they were denied the opportunity to listen to a debate on policy or to express their preference.

3 Theresa May has not faced the wider electorate as party leader. This may weaken her democratic legitimacy. This is a problem also faced by several past prime ministers who became party leader and head of government without a general election to confirm their position. These included James Callaghan, Labour (1976), John Major, Conservative (1990), and Gordon Brown, Labour (2007).

Why did Mrs May win?

Theresa May won with very little effective opposition and the Conservative Party let out a collective sigh of relief that there had been no damaging and divisive leadership contest. Their pleasure was heightened by the knowledge that the Labour Party was about to conduct a hugely divisive leadership ballot.

But it was not as simple as avoiding a contest. Theresa May had a number of significant advantages over her opponents. Among them were these:

- Her potentially most dangerous opponent, former mayor of London and leading 'Leave' campaigner Boris Johnson, withdrew just before the contest opened. It is widely reported that he had agreed to run as long as Michael Gove would support him, but that Gove betrayed him by standing for the office himself. Without Gove's support, Johnson felt his chance had gone and he withdrew.

- It was widely believed in the Conservative Party that she had been a successful home secretary. This is not entirely borne out by the facts. In her six years in office, she had presided over growing net immigration into the UK when her party was promising dramatic reductions. At the same time, the prison population remained stubbornly high, at over 85,000 in 2010–15, despite repeated promises to bring this figure down. Nevertheless, she was seen as a strong, decisive home secretary.

- Though she declared herself for 'Remain' in the EU referendum campaign, it was well known that she was not especially enthusiastic and so could stand in a central position, able to unite both sides in the EU debate.

- Seen as being slightly on the right in the party, she was nevertheless viewed as a consensus politician, seeking widespread agreement rather than major policy conflicts.

- Though she did not have to face them in the election as it turned out, she undoubtedly enjoyed widespread support among the ordinary members of the Conservative Party. She was, indeed, often regarded as a 'model Tory', a true Conservative but untouched by any extreme ideological positions.

- She was educated at a state school and came from a middle-of-the-road, middle-class background, so removing the charge against much of the Conservative leadership of being from a privileged élite that could not understand the problems of ordinary people.

By contrast, her opponents were seen as either inexperienced (Leadsom, Crabb), untrustworthy (Gove) or too ideologically driven (Fox, a prominent right-winger).

In summary, therefore, Mrs May's elevation to prime minister was the result of a series of events, all of them unpredictable:

- The outcome of the referendum, to leave the EU, was totally unexpected.
- David Cameron's resignation was not predicted.
- Boris Johnson surprisingly withdrew from the leadership contest.
- None of the other candidates for the leadership mounted a serious challenge.

What are Mrs May's political beliefs?

In her first speech as prime minister, Mrs May shocked everyone. With her reputation as a right-winger, it was not expected that she should express such liberal and social democratic views. A key extract from the speech, delivered in Downing Street on 13 July 2016, is shown in Box 3.1. It contains most of the surprising sentiments that she expressed.

Box 3.1 **Theresa May's first speech as prime minister**

...it means we believe in the union, the precious, precious bond between England, Scotland, Wales and Northern Ireland. But it means something else that is just as important, it means we believe in a union not just between the nations of the United Kingdom, but between all our citizens, every one of us, whoever we are and wherever we are from. **That means fighting against the burning injustice that if you're born poor you will die on average nine years earlier than others. If you're black, you're treated more harshly by the criminal justice system than if you're white. If you're a white, working-class boy, you're less likely than anybody else in Britain to go to university. If you're at a state school, you're less likely to reach the top professions than if you're educated privately. If you're a woman, you will earn less than a man. If you suffer from mental health problems, there's not enough help to hand. If you're young you'll find it harder than ever to own your own home.**

But the mission to make Britain a country that works for everyone means more than fighting these injustices. If you're from an ordinary working-class family, life is much harder than many people in Westminster realise. **You have a job but you don't always have job security. You have your own home but you worry about paying the mortgage. You can just manage but you worry about the cost of living and getting your kids into a good school...The government I lead will be driven, not by the interests of the privileged few but by yours...When we pass new laws we'll listen not to the mighty, but to you. When it comes to taxes we'll prioritise not the wealthy, but you...**

Such a speech could have been delivered by Barack Obama in the USA or by a Labour leader in Britain. It contained the following ideals (shown in bold in Box 3.1):

- formal equality for minority groups
- equality of opportunity for all

- spreading wealth more widely
- fair taxation
- the end of the advantages of artificial privilege

It was immediately branded a 'One Nation' speech, but it contained so many ideas about social justice that it could be described as a vision of social democracy.

But in case anyone thought she might be a faint-hearted liberal, Mrs May immediately showed her steel. She removed a large proportion of Cameron's old cabinet, dismissing the chancellor of the exchequer, George Osborne, the education secretary, Nicky Morgan, the policy adviser, Oliver Letwyn, and the justice secretary, Michael Gove. It was clear that this was to be *her* cabinet. She even promoted her erstwhile rival, Boris Johnson, to the post of foreign secretary, a move that shocked the political establishment.

How will she manage Brexit?

Mrs May appointed three prominent members of the Leave campaign to lead the UK's negotiation out of the EU. These were:
- Boris Johnson, foreign secretary
- David Davis, secretary for leaving the European Union
- Liam Fox, international trade secretary

At first it appeared that she was going to leave negotiations to this triumvirate. However, it soon became clear that this was an illusion. Having met many prominent European heads of government and then attended the G20 conference in September 2016, it was clear that she was setting the agenda for Brexit as well as future relations with China. She defied the wishes of the 'Leave' campaign by ruling out a 'points system' for future immigration, preferring a system of work permits, and made it clear she would be negotiating with European leaders on the UK's Brexit strategy.

What kind of prime minister will Theresa May be?

It is too early to determine what kind of prime minister she will turn out to be. However, there is some evidence based on her past record as an MP and as a minister, as well as her first few months in office. Her characteristics appear to include these:
- She looks like being a 'controlling' prime minister, preferring to concern herself with a wide range of policy areas rather than leaving them to her ministers.
- She clearly prides herself on being a difficult, tough negotiator. Her reputation suggests she can be very stubborn and difficult to dislodge from her entrenched views. In this respect she has been compared to Margaret Thatcher.
- She has positioned herself firmly as a 'One Nation' Tory, determined to ensure that government policies work for the whole community.
- She is a 'hawk' on foreign policy and domestic security. She has shown herself in favour of foreign interventions, for example in Syria and Iraq, and is willing to sacrifice human rights for the sake of anti-terrorist measures.

- She is socially liberal on the whole, having voted in favour of gay marriage and presenting herself as a champion of women's rights. However, some believe this aspect of her politics does not run very deep.
- On the economy she announced herself as a dominant figure by making herself chair of the important cabinet economic committee. She has signalled an end to deep austerity and proposes expansionary policies to create more jobs and improve industrial productivity. She supports an 'industrial policy' to replace the free-market policies of her predecessors.

Time will tell, but early indications suggest that Theresa May is willing to reset Conservative policy completely. Dismissing so many prominent ministers is clear evidence of this stance. On the whole, however, she is perhaps best summed up as a typical 'One Nation' Tory. This suggests she is intent on uniting the nation and on avoiding excessive ideological positions.

What does Theresa May's election tell us about political leadership?

Any party leader has to consider three groups when seeking election and, having been elected, he or she must seek to retain their support. The three groups are:

- **The members of the parliamentary party.** These are the members who will enable her to govern effectively. Without their support it will be difficult for her to implement her plans. Theresa May won overwhelming support from Conservative MPs, so she is in a good position. MPs tend to be relatively moderate, so extreme positions need to be avoided.
- **The members of the party up and down the country.** These are also known as 'grass-roots' members. Mrs May did not have to face them, as all her opponents withdrew. The research suggests that she would have won the vote among members comfortably, but not necessarily if she had faced Boris Johnson. In contrast, the rivals to Jeremy Corbyn's leadership of Labour have found that party members support him in large numbers. Grass-roots members tend to be more extreme, on the left or right in their views. If they have the final say, therefore, moderate candidates are at a disadvantage.
- **Those who vote for the party normally.** These are the most moderate group of all. Here Theresa May has a huge advantage over Jeremy Corbyn in that she is popular with Tory voters all over the country, while he does not enjoy such support among Labour voters.

The system for electing a Conservative leader goes a long way to ensuring that all three groups will be happy with the outcome. Theresa May does face a dissident right-wing group of MPs and may face problems if the UK cannot negotiate a satisfactory deal with the EU post-Brexit, but she has made an effective start and is clearly determined to control the whole party.

Conclusion

At the beginning of this chapter we asked how and why Theresa May became prime minister. The answer to these two questions can be summarised as follows:

- She became prime minister because her predecessor unexpectedly resigned as a result of an unexpected event. She won as a result of a leadership electoral system that favoured her.
- She won for two main reasons. One was that her most serious potential rival — Boris Johnson — withdrew before the contest began. The second was that she was the right person in the right place at the right time. She was a typical 'One Nation' Tory, which her party likes and which meant that she was a uniting figure rather than a divisive one, she was an experienced and well-respected minister, and the opportunity came at the perfect moment in her political career. It is, interestingly, almost the same coincidence of events that brought Tony Blair to the Labour leadership in 1994.

Exam focus

To consolidate your knowledge of this chapter, answer the following questions:

1 Assess the effectiveness of the way in which the Conservative Party elects its leader.
2 How democratic is the way in which the Conservative Party elects its leader?
3 Discuss the importance of patronage for the prime minister.
4 What is meant by the term 'One-Nation Conservative'?
5 In what senses is Theresa May 'lucky' to have become prime minister?

Chapter 4

David Cameron: a verdict on his premiership

Context

The prominent Conservative politician of the 1960s and 1970s, Enoch Powell, once famously asserted that 'all political careers end in failure'. When David Cameron announced his intention to resign both as Conservative leader and prime minister the day after the EU referendum resulted in the decision to leave, Powell's words might have been ringing in his ears. It was indeed a dramatic and unexpected fall from power. Ironically, the man on whose style Cameron had modelled himself — Tony Blair — fell from grace equally dramatically in 2007. Blair's great error was to take the UK into the war with Iraq that had such disastrous consequences for the Middle East and the Western world. Cameron's was a double failure. First, he called a referendum when he really did not need to, and secondly, he led the campaign that could not persuade the electorate to stay in the EU.

Until his sudden fall, Cameron's record as a prime minister was decidedly mixed. His government could claim several successes and, economically at least, could claim to have left the country in better shape than how he found it. But there were also failures and, in the end, like Blair, he left a party that had lost confidence in him.

Cameron's road to power

The rise of David Cameron is shown below in a brief timeline of his life and career:

1966	Born in London.
1973–84	Privately educated at prep school and Eton.
1985	Started at Oxford University.
1988	Obtained a first-class degree in Philosophy, Politics and Economics.
1988–94	Worked in the Conservative Party Research Department, from 1991 advising the prime minister (John Major), chancellor of the exchequer (Norman Lamont) and home secretary (Michael Howard).
1994–2001	Worked in corporate affairs (partly as a political lobbyist) for media company Carlton Communications.
2001	Won the safe Conservative seat of Witney near Oxford and entered Parliament.
2003–5	Served in a variety of minor posts in the shadow Conservative government.
2005	Elected Conservative Party leader following the Conservative defeat at the 2005 general election and the resignation of his predecessor, Michael Howard. His candidacy was supported by Boris Johnson (an old school friend from Eton), George Osborne (a close political ally) and former Conservative leader, William Hague.
2010	After the general election he became prime minister, leading a coalition government with the Liberal Democrats.
2015	Against the odds, he won an overall majority in the general election and formed a majority government.
2016	Resigned following defeat in the referendum on UK membership of the European Union. Later he also resigned as an MP and left politics.

Up to a point it was a perfect political story. Cameron had a brilliant career at Eton and Oxford, worked both in political research at the very centre of power and then in business, and won a very safe parliamentary seat. He was, though, catapulted into power with very little senior experience, never having been a minister or a front-bench spokesman. He was also very young when he became prime minister at the age of 44, the youngest for nearly 200 years.

What were Cameron's political ideals?

In many ways David Cameron was a very typical conservative, pursuing many of the ideals of his predecessors over two centuries. Among these traits were the following:

- He had maintained an instinct to reduce taxation.
- He sought to reduce the role and size of the state and to replace many public sector providers with private sector enterprises.

- He pursued an active foreign policy in an attempt to maintain Britain's influence and status in the world.
- He strongly defended the forces of law and order and placed a high priority on the security of the state in the face of international terrorism.
- He was a unionist who strongly defended the unity of the United Kingdom.
- He showed a preference for policies that would unite the community rather than divide it.
- He remained suspicious of reform of the political system and resisted strong demands for significant constitutional reform — for example, of the electoral system and the House of Lords.
- Despite his resistance to constitutional reform he did accept that society was ready for the liberalisation of laws on gay marriage and the strengthening of laws against race hatred. In other words, he accepted the natural, organic development of a more tolerant and diverse society.
- A defender of property rights, he refused to interfere significantly in property markets and saw the inexorable rise in property prices as a largely positive development.

In addition to these conservative instincts, Cameron sought to define himself in terms of three ideals — the 'Big Society', One Nationism and social liberalism.

The 'Big Society'

The 'Big Society' was an attempt by David Cameron to carve out a distinct identity. He had seen how successful Tony Blair's 'Third Way' had been in the 1990s and thought to emulate it. There can be little doubt that David Cameron was inspired by the ideas of Edmund Burke. Burke (1729–97) is often described as the 'father' of conservatism. In his analysis of how disorder or dictatorship was to be avoided, he referred to what he called the 'little platoons' of society. These were local groups of citizens who were politically and economically active, and who maintained social cohesion and gave people a sense of identity which could not be provided by the centralised state. The little platoons could act as a guardian against the excessive power of the state.

The modern equivalent envisaged by Cameron in the current age was to consist of a network of groups such as faith groups, community societies, private companies, parent organisations and charities. In practice, the modern platoons would engage in such activities as setting up new free schools, bidding to provide local authority services, campaigning for environmental causes, establishing conservation groups and setting up charitable trusts to provide subsidised housing or social care. By taking responsibility for such activities and replacing over-reliance on the state, the theory of the 'Big Society' is that communities will thrive and opportunity will be spread more widely.

One Nationism

This has two aspects. One is a determination that the United Kingdom should remain together as one single family. In practice, this means resisting the influence of nationalism, which flourishes largely in Scotland. The second is to prevent the gap in living standards between the prosperous south and the depressed north widening further and perhaps to reduce the differences. The main practical application of this was the creation of a 'Northern Powerhouse' (also promoted by George Osborne) to improve infrastructure in the north.

Social liberalism

Though very clearly a conservative, David Cameron was something of a liberal where social affairs were concerned. He supported the progress in gay rights exemplified by the introduction of same-sex marriage. He also introduced a significant increase in the provision of nursery care for pre-school children. In secondary education, he resisted calls for the extension of selective grammar schools (which Theresa May supports) in his party, preferring to see opportunity spread through all schools.

Cameron's critics will argue that, though he paid lip service to these three philosophies, he actually achieved little. Within three years the 'Big Society' idea had withered, Scottish nationalism burgeoned, threatening the union, the gap in living standards between wealthy and poor widened and opportunities for the young continued to narrow. On the other hand, Cameron's instinct for tolerance and equal rights has been borne out by action.

A positive view of David Cameron's premiership

In *Cameron at 10: The Inside Story*, published in 2015, historian and biographer Anthony Seldon presented a largely positive review of Cameron's premiership. Among Cameron's achievements identified by Seldon are these:

- He developed a more inclusive vision of Britain than any other Conservative prime minister, taking up the cause of the gay community, women, ethnic minorities and the low-paid.
- He brought the Conservatives back into power after 13 years out of office in 2010.
- He led a coalition government — which it was widely believed could not last long — for five years and then won an election outright for his party.
- He succeeded in introducing gay marriage despite opposition from within his own party.
- He preserved the commitment that Britain should devote at least 0.7% of its national income to overseas aid, again despite fierce opposition from the Conservative right wing.
- Although he and the chancellor missed their targets in government debt reduction, he did succeed in bringing the nation's finances more under control (adapted from the *Guardian*, 15 July 2016).

To add to Seldon's list, it can be argued that Cameron shielded many families on low incomes from the worst effects of the austerity programme introduced to bring down government debt. This was done by introducing a much increased minimum wage (the 'living wage') and acceding to Liberal Democrat demands to raise the level at which people start paying tax, so taking millions of them out of paying tax altogether.

In education too, he presided over a period of steadily rising standards in schools and introduced a free school programme which aimed to increase diversity in education and to put some power back into the hands of parents.

Seldon also points out that Cameron was a risk-taker. This seemed to work when he was confronting opposition from within his own party, but sometimes failed when it came to external forces. The apparent failure of his Libya policy and the outcome of the EU referendum are the two key examples, explained further below. Leaving this positive account, we should also remember that Cameron's decision to allow the Scots a referendum on independence in 2014 was a major success as the result kept the United Kingdom together — for the time being at least.

A negative perspective on David Cameron

At the same time that Anthony Seldon was praising Cameron, historian Selina Todd wrote a rather more negative account. Her main criticisms were these:

- He failed to tackle the problem of excessive wealth being retained in the hands of a select few.
- Though he won the Scottish independence referendum, the result has been greater powers being transferred to Scotland, while the EU referendum has led to renewed demands for independence, threatening the union.
- His policy in Libya proved to be a disaster almost on a scale with Tony Blair's Iraq adventure. While his decision to help anti-government rebels with air power was successful in the short term, and the much reviled dictatorship of Colonel Gaddafi was brought to an end, like Blair and US President George Bush Jr in Iraq, there was no plan for restoring order in the country and the result in both cases has been bloodshed and chaos.
- Above all, his decision to allow a referendum on EU membership was an error of judgement, driven not be his own conviction but by a desire to gain political control over his party's Eurosceptic wing and to undermine UKIP.
- He led the 'Remain' campaign to defeat.

Two further criticisms can be levelled at David Cameron. The first is the failure to meet the government's targets on government debt reduction. The government's austerity programme, which many claim has done serious damage to public services, failed to achieve its aim, possibly as a result of the government's reluctance to raise taxes. Indeed, Cameron can be accused of presiding over a decline in the NHS and in the provision of social care, as well as the erosion of many welfare benefits and the near collapse of subsidised housing. Secondly, his flagship philosophy of the 'Big Society' proved to be virtually stillborn. Other than the flourishing free school programme, little evidence can be found of Big Society initiatives.

Conclusion

What does David Cameron's experience tell us about the office of prime minister? As we have seen, the experience of David Cameron has been mixed. However, we can discern a number of consistent themes which can inform us about both the extent of and limits to prime ministerial power. We can therefore divide these conclusions into two sections.

Strengths

- Though he was supported by the chancellor of the exchequer and the Treasury, it was clear that the prime minister was chief economic policy maker. Cameron was determined that the UK would make inroads into public sector debt even if this meant a measure of austerity, and he firmly led the government's strategy.
- As long as he maintained the support of an inner group of ministers (Osborne, May, Gove, Letwin), he could dominate government.
- Parliamentary performance was important. Cameron learned how to handle Parliament and this gave him great authority.

Weaknesses

- Without a decisive parliamentary majority, he was always in a fragile position. Cameron was forced into actions he might not have undertaken had he enjoyed more parliamentary support. The prime example was the calling of the EU referendum, though his actions in Syria and Libya were also constrained by a non-compliant Parliament.
- The prime minister remained vulnerable to events outside his control. In particular, Brexit was a totally unexpected development. In addition, he found it difficult to respond to the overwhelming refugee crisis that emerged in 2014.
- Ultimately, every prime minister stands alone at the apex of government. He or she is responsible for the performance of government. So, when the UK voted to leave the EU, David Cameron could not transfer responsibility to anyone else. He had to take responsibility and so he resigned.

Once again, Enoch Powell's assertion about political careers ending in failure was proved to be accurate.

Exam focus

To consolidate your knowledge of this chapter, answer the following questions:

1. What are the main limitations to the power of the UK prime minister?
2. To what extent are prime ministers vulnerable to events beyond their control?
3. What is meant by the term 'One-Nation conservatism'?
4. Why was David Cameron sometimes described as a 'liberal conservative'?
5. In what senses was David Cameron a 'typical conservative'?

Chapter 5

Brexit: will it lead to the break-up of the United Kingdom?

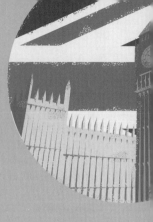

Exam success

The up-to-date facts, examples and arguments in this chapter will help you to produce good-quality answers in your AS unit tests in the following areas of the specifications.

Edexcel	AQA	OCR
Unit 2	**Unit 2**	**Unit F852**
The constitution	Multi-level governance	The constitution

Context

In the national referendum on the UK's membership of the European Union in June 2016, as we saw in Chapter 2, the different parts of the UK came to different conclusions. This chapter examines whether these differences threaten the very existence of the United Kingdom or whether the unity of the kingdom is likely to survive.

The people of Northern Ireland voted to remain in the European Union by 56% to 44%. All the major parties in Northern Ireland campaigned for a Remain vote and UKIP has little presence there, so it was no great surprise. However, Sinn Fein, the main opposition party, immediately called for a 'border referendum' to gauge opinion on the reunification of Ireland, to be achieved within the European Union.

After Scotland voted by 55% to 45% to remain in the United Kingdom in 2014, it was assumed that the issue of independence would be put into hibernation, at least for a generation. Indeed, even the Scottish National Party seemed to accept that it was not going to happen in the foreseeable future. Then everything changed again. The scenario is relatively straightforward. In the 2016 referendum on UK membership of the European Union, the Scottish voters chose to remain in the EU by a significantly large majority of 62% to 38%. It was therefore clear that the rest of the UK, England in particular, was forcing Scotland out of the EU against its will.

Any hopes that Scotland might, after Brexit, be able to negotiate some sort of separate relationship with the EU were immediately dashed; there could be no special trade deal, no separate agreements on the movement of people and labour, and no hope of continuation of EU development grants. Scotland would have to leave along with the rest of the UK. This immediately sparked fresh demands for independence. The whole landscape had changed since 2014, the nationalists argued.

Wales, however, followed the rest of the United Kingdom by supporting Leave by 53% to 47%. UKIP was influential in Wales, which may have been a factor, along with economic stagnation in several Welsh regions, some of which was blamed on the European Union and excessive levels of immigration. The result was a blow to Plaid Cymru, the Welsh nationalist party, which campaigned strongly to Remain.

The situation in each of the three countries is examined below.

Northern Ireland

The issue of Northern Ireland's place in the United Kingdom after Brexit is complicated by the fact that it shares a border with the Republic of Ireland. While both the UK and Ireland are EU members this border is open, with goods and people flowing freely between the two. This ended a long history of smuggling — to avoid UK taxation — that used to take place before Ireland was an EU member. When the UK leaves the EU, however, this border may well close again. There are no guarantees that the UK will be able to negotiate free trade and free movement of people with the Irish Republic.

The Republicans (Irish nationalists) in Northern Ireland therefore see this as an opportunity to renew the question of a unified Ireland, taking Northern Ireland out of the United Kingdom. After the Brexit vote, Sinn Fein president Gerry Adams claimed that the Leave vote was invalid in Northern Ireland and called for an all-Ireland referendum on the question of Irish reunification. Given Northern Ireland's long history of inter-communal violence, especially between the 1970s and 1990s, this was a potentially inflammatory statement. To nobody's surprise, the Unionists urged the community to accept the Leave vote.

Northern Ireland's deputy first minister, Martin McGuinness (of Sinn Fein), said, soon after the EU referendum:

> The British government now has no democratic mandate to represent the views of the North in any future negotiations with the European Union and I do believe that there is a democratic imperative for a 'border poll' to be held.

Meanwhile UK Northern Ireland secretary, Theresa Villiers, rejected the idea of an Irish referendum out of hand. She argued that opinion *within* Northern Ireland was firmly against Irish reunification. Nevertheless some commentators in Northern Ireland were suggesting that, if European Union farm subsidies

are withdrawn and if the UK fails to negotiate an advantageous trade deal after Brexit, even Unionists might also opt for Irish unification. To illustrate the concerns in the province, thousands of Northern Ireland residents have applied for Irish citizenship so that they will have the option of crossing the border into the Republic of Ireland and living in the European Union in the future.

An opinion poll conducted by the *Belfast Telegraph* in July 2016 and covering the whole of Ireland, the North — part of the UK — plus the independent Republic of Ireland, demonstrated that the vast majority of Irish people wish to see a united Ireland, i.e. that Northern Ireland should leave the UK: 74% favoured a referendum and 70% said they would vote for a united Ireland if such a referendum were held. Unlike in Scotland, there are no serious calls for Northern Ireland to be independent on its own. Constitutional experts, however, point out that a referendum conducted partly in a foreign country would have no authority in the UK, where parliament is sovereign.

But the real test of a possible change in the constitutional status of Northern Ireland would be a referendum of the people of Northern Ireland themselves. Opinion polls carried out as recently as 2013 and 2014 by Ipsos Mori showed that at least twice as many residents would vote to stay a part of the UK as would vote to leave. Even the Catholic community, which is more sympathetic to Irish reunification, split evenly for and against the proposal. The Catholic population in Northern Ireland is growing faster than non-Catholics and young people are more sympathetic to Irish unity, but, at the current rate of change, it will take many decades before opinion moves towards unification. However, the Brexit vote might have brought such a situation slightly closer.

Scotland

In the campaign before the 2016 elections to the Scottish Parliament, the Scottish National Party manifesto stated that there would only be a second referendum on Scottish independence (following the 2014 negative vote) if there were 'a significant and material change in the circumstances that prevailed in 2014'. Speaking the day after the EU referendum, Nicola Sturgeon held a press conference at which she referred back to this part of the SNP manifesto, saying:

> It is, therefore, a statement of the obvious that a second referendum must be on the table, and it is on the table...It looks highly likely that there will now be a second referendum on Scottish independence.

A month later, however, Ms Sturgeon had moderated her calls for such a referendum, as her speech to the Institute of Public Policy Research on 25 July 2016, reported in Box 5.1, shows.

Nicola Sturgeon on a possible new Scottish referendum

That brings me, of course, to the question of independence. I'm a lifelong nationalist — but I said in the immediate aftermath of the EU referendum that, in seeking to chart a way forward for Scotland, independence was not my starting point. That remains the case. Protecting Scotland's interests is my starting point and I will explore all options to do so. But I am equally clear about this — if we find that our interests can't be protected in a UK context, independence must be one of those options and Scotland must have the right to consider it. That is why we will take the preparatory steps to ensure that this option is open to the Scottish Parliament if the Scottish Parliament considers it necessary.

It was clear that the problems of clearing the way for a second Scottish referendum were considerable. In addition, Nicola Sturgeon might have become aware of how opinion on independence was moving in Scotland. Table 5.1 shows four results of opinion polls conducted by the polling organisation, What Scotland Thinks (**whatscotlandthinks.org**).

Table 5.1 Four opinion polls on Scottish independence*

Date of poll	Yes to independence (%)	No to independence (%)
26 June 2016	53	47
25 July 2016	47	53
31 August 2016	47	53
15 September 2016	48	52
2014 referendum result	**45**	**55**

* 'Don't know' responses not included.

We can see that there was an immediate knee-jerk reaction to the Brexit vote and that a majority would have voted for independence at that time, but this reaction has cooled since and there is now a majority shown against independence. The poll results remain closer than the actual independence referendum result, but they are certainly not encouraging for Scottish nationalists, hence the change in Nicola Sturgeon's tone.

Meeting Nicola Sturgeon in July 2016, the new UK prime minister, Theresa May, promised to take Scotland's interests into consideration when negotiating the UK's exit from the EU, but completely ruled out a second referendum on Scottish independence. She told a press conference on 14 July:

As far as I'm concerned, the Scottish people have had their vote, they voted in 2014 and a very clear message came through. Both the United Kingdom and the Scottish government said they would abide by that.

Wales

One thing can be said for certain, which is that there will be no referendum on Welsh independence any time soon. Opinion in Wales has long been decisively against independence and Brexit has done nothing to change that situation. The fact that a majority of Welsh voters chose to leave the EU is also a testimony to the lack of appetite for independence from the UK.

There is something of an irony in Wales' decision to leave the EU along with the rest of the UK, as the country has a good deal to lose from Brexit. There is no certainty that generous EU subsidies to farmers and grants for economic development will be replaced by like-for-like UK aid. Even so, we can say with great confidence that Wales is as firmly a part of the United Kingdom as it ever was.

Yet Plaid Cymru, the party of Welsh nationalism, remained defiant. Its leader Leanne Wood, writing in the *Guardian* on 29 June 2016, shortly after the referendum result, suggested that Welsh independence was 'back on the agenda' (see Box 5.2). Relatively few in Wales, though, share her view as yet.

Box 5.2   Leanne Wood on Brexit and Welsh independence

This week has placed an independent Wales back on the agenda. This is not because of events of our own choosing, but because Brexit means that the UK could well be no more. This is not an attempt to say that Wales is in the same position as Scotland. We are not. We didn't vote to remain. I am, though, very clear that Wales' future is bound up with that of the other UK countries. If other nations are advocating this path, why would we in Wales not even be debating it as an option?

A footnote on London

In some ways London and the southeast of England have more cause to look towards independence following Brexit than any other region. London as a whole voted by virtually 60% to 40% to remain in the European Union. In some more affluent areas 70% voted to remain. Furthermore, there have long been complaints that London and the southeast region contribute much more than other regions, in terms of income and tax per head, to the wealth of the UK, and take far less in terms of government investment and welfare payments. In other words, London subsidises the rest of the country substantially. Now, as a further blow to national unity, it is to be pulled out of the European Union against its will. In addition, there are fears that London will suffer disproportionately from Brexit, as it is so internationally connected.

No one is seriously proposing that London should try to secede from the United Kingdom, but the situation does demonstrate again how London-centric the UK is and how unbalanced is the distribution of wealth and income. This makes devolution and the need to re-balance the economy towards outer regions more of a priority. If the gap continues to grow between London and the rest of the UK, there may be serious repercussions in terms of cultural and economic disunity.

Conclusion

UK politics is in a state of great change and uncertainty, to say the least, so drawing conclusions about the post-Brexit world is fraught with difficulty. We cannot predict the future relationship the UK may have with the EU and, indeed, the rest of the world. If the UK government cannot or will not replace the subsidies its poorer regions now receive from the EU, there may be great unrest in Scotland, Wales and Northern Ireland. Worse still, if there is a significant economic slowdown or even a recession in the wake of Brexit, dissatisfaction will grow everywhere and the decision to leave the EU will look increasingly reckless. However, the evidence, as it currently stands, suggests that the United Kingdom will survive for some time to come.

There *is* growing nationalist sentiment in Scotland and Northern Ireland, but it seems unlikely that it will be strong enough to lead to independence just yet.

Exam focus

To consolidate your knowledge of this chapter, answer the following questions:

1 Why has nationalism grown so substantially in recent years in the national regions of the UK?
2 What are the main elements of the case put forward for Scottish independence?
3 Why did the national regions of the UK have more interest in EU membership than most of England?
4 How has the distribution of sovereignty in the UK been affected by the EU referendum?
5 Distinguish between the Unionist and the Republican positions on sovereignty in Northern Ireland.

Chapter 6

The Labour Party: time to split?

Exam success

The up-to-date facts, examples and arguments in this chapter will help you to produce good-quality answers in your AS unit tests in the following areas of the specifications.

Edexcel	AQA	OCR
Unit 1	**Unit 1**	**Unit F851**
Party policies and ideas	Political parties	Political parties

Context

Political parties have a number of different stakeholders. The five main groups are:

- the elected members of parliament
- those who normally vote for the party
- the ordinary members of the party in constituencies (and unions in Labour's case)
- party activists — those who work hard for the party in constituencies
- the leadership group

When a party is unified and has a strong sense of common purpose, all five of these groups will probably share a similar vision. This occurred in the Conservative Party under Margaret Thatcher in the 1980s and in Labour under Tony Blair in the late 1990s and early this century. From time to time, however, such unity can prove elusive.

It is normal for the activists in a party to hold more radical or extreme views and for the voters to be the most moderate supporters. However, since Jeremy Corbyn became Labour leader, there has been considerable internal disunity. The leadership group and the activists are very radical in their socialist and quasi-socialist views, but they are at odds with moderate party members, most MPs and most Labour voters. In other words, the *members* of the Labour Party hold one set of beliefs but most voters share another. Most MPs, not surprisingly, share the more moderate views of the voters.

This chapter examines how Labour got itself into this position and asks where it can go from here.

The story so far

The story of how Jeremy Corbyn became leader of the Labour Party reads something like a Shakespeare play, divided into five acts. It certainly resembles one of the bard's history plays or perhaps — depending on the final outcome — one of his tragedies. It is certainly not a comedy! This play is full of typical Shakespearean themes — treachery, irony, ambition and warfare.

Act 1: the story of the two brothers

In 2010, following his failure to win the general election of that year for Labour, Labour leader Gordon Brown fell on his sword and resigned. In the election for the leadership that followed, all the contenders fell away in the early ballots, leaving two brothers to fight it out — David and Ed Miliband. It was thought that David was the favourite and that perhaps his younger brother, Ed, might stand down in his favour. However, in an act often described as treachery, Ed refused to give way and won the election.

At that time the leadership was determined by an electoral college. Three sections of the party voted separately. These were the MPs, the trade unions attached to Labour and the ordinary party members from the constituencies out in the country. David won the MPs' vote and was most popular among members, but Ed won the trade union section's vote. By an arithmetical device, Ed was the winner because his percentage of the union vote was so high that it counted for more than David's narrow win in the other two sections. So Ed became leader and David went into exile, to head up a large international refugee organisation.

Many of the Labour courtiers said the election of Ed had been unfair, so they asked for a change in the system. Ed granted their wish. The rules were changed so that any new leader would be elected by a straightforward election among the members on a one person, one vote basis. Furthermore, in an act of daring audacity, the rules were also changed to allow people to become 'registered supporters' and pay just £3 for the right to vote in a leadership election. Without realising what it had done, the party accepted the new rules. The far-reaching consequences of the change were not recognised.

Act 2: the leader is dead, long live the leader!

In dramas like this, characters who commit acts of 'treachery' are expected to receive their just deserts. So, when Ed Miliband lost the 2015 general election, he had to go. Like Gordon Brown, his predecessor, Ed resigned. Unlike his brother, however, he stayed in parliament where he could survey the results of his leadership election reforms. At this point, irony took over. One of the new rules was that, in order to take part in the leadership election, a candidate would need to be nominated by at least 15% of the party's MPs. This represented at least 35 members.

Now a new character entered the scene. Veteran backbench left-winger, Jeremy Corbyn, joined the fray. Little notice was taken of his bid. Indeed, he was struggling to find 35 MPs to nominate him. A few moderate MPs, including former deputy

party leader Margaret Beckett, actually nominated Corbyn even though they had no intention of voting for him. How could this be? The answer was that the other candidates all had similar political positions: in other words, there was a lack of choice. So, in order to provide a good range of candidates and to promote a full policy debate in the party, it was thought desirable that Corbyn should be able to stand. He achieved his 35 nominations and entered the first round.

The main characters failed to notice, meanwhile, that large numbers of people were becoming registered supporters. Party membership grew rapidly. It all seemed very encouraging, all these new people taking an interest in the contest. Perhaps, they thought, Labour did have a rosy future. All that was needed was a new leader and Labour would become a force again, especially as the Conservative government had a small majority of only 12 in the Commons.

As the contest got under way, the opinion polls were indicating a startling phenomenon. Corbyn was ahead! He might even win. Large numbers of moderate Labour MPs expressed their dismay at the prospect of a Corbyn victory. 'He will make the party unelectable,' they cried. 'We will not support him even if he wins,' they warned. But it was all in vain. Corbyn won on the first ballot with 59.5% of the members' vote (see Table 6.1). It was a crushing victory. The irony — that several MPs had nominated him just for the sake of balance and now were horrified by his victory — dawned on everyone. So, Labour had a new leader and he appeared to be a genuine socialist! The new members of the party, many of them young, all of them radical idealists, were exultant.

Table 6.1 Results of the Labour leadership election, 2015

Candidate	Votes	% of vote
Jeremy Corbyn	251,417	59.5
Andy Burnham	80,462	19.0
Yvette Cooper	71,928	17.0
Liz Kendall	18,857	4.5

Act 3: Jeremy's revenge and a plot to oust him

As expected, Corbyn appointed a shadow cabinet packed with many of his own supporters. Many of those who had campaigned so strongly against him were removed from their positions in the party. Notably, his faithful lieutenant, John McDonnell joined him as shadow chancellor. However, he also appointed moderate members of the party as a balance to his close supporters. Tom Watson, the elected deputy leader, had to stay despite the fact that he was on the opposite wing of the party to the new leader. Corbyn also appointed Andy Burnham, perhaps his closest rival in the leadership contest, to the shadow cabinet.

As 2015 turned into 2016, discontent with Corbyn grew among MPs. The media also turned dramatically against him, branding him unpatriotic, weak and out of touch with popular opinion. The last straw occurred when the UK voted to leave the EU in the 23 June referendum. Corbyn was accused of campaigning unenthusiastically on the 'Remain' side and was suspected of being a closet 'Leave' supporter. Many of Corbyn's shadow cabinet resigned; so many left that he found it difficult to find enough MPs willing to serve under him. It was clear that there was now a widespread plot to remove him. All the plotters needed was a champion to challenge him. Step forward Labour veteran Angela Eagle and a little-known Welsh newcomer, Owen Smith, the MP for Pontypridd.

Act 4: a white knight appears on the horizon

A leadership challenge was thrown down and Corbyn accepted it. Both sides retired to assemble their battle plan. Eagle soon dropped out; it was clear that Smith had more support than her. She would throw her lot in with him and campaign against Corbyn.

The challenger based some of his hopes on the fact that the party's governing body, the National Executive Committee, raised the fee for becoming a registered supporter from £3 to £25 for this second leadership election. That, the anti-Corbynites hoped, would deter most of the young enthusiasts. They were wrong: 180,000 new supporters paid their £25. Smith knew his bid for power was doomed. Corbyn's existing supporters stuck with him on the whole, even though Smith styled himself as being, like Corbyn, on the left of the party. The enduring support that Corbyn enjoyed, together with even more new members, gave him an easy win with an increased vote of 61.8%.

Smith, soundly beaten, retreated back to Wales. A triumphant Corbyn promptly created a new shadow cabinet composed almost exclusively of his own supporters. Even Rosie Winterton, the party's former chief whip — and its last hope, many claimed, of promoting unity — was dismissed. While the deputy leader, Tom Watson, silently brooded, Andy Burnham, another prospective unifier, withdrew to stand for election as mayor of Manchester in 2017. Jeremy Corbyn had defeated all his opponents and was established in power with a second mandate from his party. But he still lacks friends in the party leadership. The plotters may have lost this second battle, but they remain on the backbenches, discontented and fretting about the apparently bleak future for the Labour Party.

Table 6.2 Results of the Labour leadership election, 2016

Candidate	Votes	% of vote
Jeremy Corbyn	313,209	61.8
Owen Smith	193,229	38.2

Act 5: the future

This part of our play is yet to be written. There are a number of different scenarios to contemplate in the months and years to come. One thing is certain, however: Labour's position is precarious. It would be rendered even more critical if Theresa

May decided to call an early election, perhaps in spring 2017. Jeremy Corbyn, having seen off his enemies in his own party, might soon have to face an even greater adversary.

Possible scenarios

Among the potential future outcomes for the Labour Party are these:

- The 'nuclear' option is that the Labour Party may simply split into two. There is a precedent for this. In 1981, many moderate members of Labour became disillusioned with the leadership of Michael Foot and his supporters. Foot held similar views to those of Corbyn. Indeed, Corbyn first became an MP (for Islington North in London) in 1983 when Foot was leader. The breakaway group formed the Social Democrat Party and entered into an alliance with the Liberal Party. However, they failed to make an electoral breakthrough in either the 1983 or 1987 general elections and so merged with the Liberals to form the Liberal Democrat Party.

- Splitting the party would be fraught with difficulty. The 'official' party would still be led by Jeremy Corbyn. A new breakaway party would have no organisation in the constituencies and would have problems organising itself in time to fight an election. Furthermore, by splitting the centre-left vote in the country, neither existing Labour nor the new party could possibly win a majority.

- Labour MPs could split into two groups inside parliament. There are no recent precedents for this, so it is difficult to predict how it might work out. The anti-Corbyn wing would be bigger and would probably form the official opposition (the speaker would have to rule on this). The pro-Corbyn wing would probably be smaller. This begs the question: what would happen at the next general election? Many MPs would not be re-selected to fight their seats; a whole new raft of pro-Corbyn candidates would probably be selected. Labour, purged of many of its moderates, would have difficulty winning enough seats to make a significant impact. There will have to be a radical change in public sentiment if a 'Corbynite' party is to challenge the Conservatives.

- Nothing might immediately happen. Labour, with a pro-Corbyn shadow cabinet, might struggle on with the moderate MPs largely acting as individuals. The party would simply cease to operate as a single unit. This would mean an ineffective, divided opposition, which many feel would be bad for democracy. Before the next election, however, some sort of long-term settlement would have to be reached.

- As things stand at the end of 2016, the least likely scenario would seem to be reconciliation between the pro- and anti-Corbyn sides of the party. This would require a great deal of compromise on both sides and there is little indication of that so far. It would also mean that the old wounds, described above, would have to be healed. The chances of Labour producing a generally agreed manifesto also look remote (see Box 6.1).

How Corbyn's ideas differ from moderate Labour opinion

Jeremy Corbyn's ideas	Moderate Labour opinion
He would introduce a 'wealth tax' on the very well off.	Taxation should be progressive but should still reward successful entrepreneurs.
Corbyn and McDonnell propose very large increases in public expenditure, funded by borrowing, for infrastructure investment.	The moderates want some expansion in spending but on a much smaller scale, as they wish to avoid excessive government debt.
The energy industries should be brought under public ownership and state control.	Industry should remain in the private sector and be subject to free market forces, though with some regulation.
Banks should be brought under close state regulation and control.	Banks should be further regulated but not controlled by government.
Trident nuclear weapons should be scrapped.	Trident should be retained and renewed.
He would have the UK leave NATO.	Moderates are committed to NATO.
He believes we should cooperate with Russia.	The USA remains the UK's main ally. Most MPs wish to confront Russia.
He would introduce controls on private rents.	There is no enthusiasm for rent control. Most members prefer to make home ownership more accessible.
He would abolish university tuition fees.	Tuition fees will have to remain in place.

Some remaining consensual ideas within Labour

- Strong support for the welfare state.
- Tighter controls on tax evasion and avoidance.
- Support for an extensive house-building programme.
- Opposition to tight immigration controls.
- Opposition to grammar schools.
- Nationalisation of the railways.
- The UK should avoid excessive involvement in Middle East conflicts.

Conclusion

Party politics in the UK is currently in a state of flux and uncertainty. Brexit has destabilised the Conservative Party, the Liberal Democrats' future is in doubt and UKIP is in a permanent state of crisis from which it may not recover. Scottish nationalism is on the march again and, of course, Labour is in turmoil. This makes it difficult to predict the future.

One thing can be said with some certainty. Parties that split are unlikely to recover from the experience for many years. Even if Labour does not split, it looks set to remain disunited for the foreseeable future. Voters traditionally do not like disunited parties. Labour discovered this between 1979 and 1997, and the Conservatives suffered in the same way from 1992 to 2010. Whatever happens, things look bleak for Labour.

Exam focus

To consolidate your knowledge of this chapter, answer the following questions:

1 How democratic is the Labour Party?
2 How and why is the Labour Party divided on ideological lines?
3 Distinguish between party members, MPs and leaders.
4 Why is parliamentary opposition currently weak in the UK and why is this a threat to democracy?
5 Why is Jeremy Corbyn considered to be a 'radical' politician?

Chapter 7

The 2016 elections to devolved administrations: does PR work?

Context

In 2016 there were elections to representative assemblies in Scotland, Wales and Northern Ireland as well as to the Greater London Assembly. In all these cases a proportional electoral system is used, although in most of them the system is hybrid, i.e. partly proportional and partly first-past-the-post (FPTP). These elections and their outcomes give us valuable clues to how the UK political system might be affected if proportional representation (PR) were used for general elections. The results of the devolved elections are shown in Tables 7.1–7.4 below. First we need a reminder of how the two electoral systems work.

How the two electoral systems work

Additional Member System (AMS)

AMS systems are used in Scotland and Wales and for the London Assembly. A version is also used in Germany. They are known as **hybrids** or **mixed systems** because they are a combination of first-past-the-post (FPTP) and a regional list system. A proportion (which varies from country to country) of the seats is awarded through FPTP. The rest are awarded according to a regional list system. This means that every voter has two votes. One is for a constituency candidate in the normal way, while the other is from a choice of party lists.

So, some of the elected representatives have a constituency to look after, while others do not. The latter have been elected from the lists and are free of constituency

responsibilities. No real distinction is made between them, though the senior party members tend to be elected from lists rather than in constituencies.

AMS is something of a compromise. It is designed to make a system *partly* proportional, but also preserves the idea of parliamentary constituencies with an MP to represent them. It helps smaller parties, but also favours the larger ones. It achieves two objectives at the same time, preserving the idea of constituencies and a constituency representative, but producing a much more proportional result than FPTP.

How AMS works in Scotland, Wales and London

- A proportion of the seats are elected using FPTP, as for UK general elections. Voters choose an individual candidate for their constituency.
- The rest of the seats are elected on the basis of regional list voting. Voters choose a list of candidates offered in their region by each party. In other words, in this case they vote for a party, not a single candidate.
- This means voters have two votes: one for an individual in the constituency and one for a party.
- There is an important variation in the regional list part of the vote. The **variable top-up system** adjusts the proportions of votes cast on the list system. This is a complex calculation, but in essence what happens is that the seats awarded from the list system are adjusted to give a more proportional result. It is known as the **D'Hondt method**.
- Parties that do less well in the constituencies (typically, Conservatives or Greens) have their proportion of list votes adjusted *upwards*. Those that do proportionally well under FPTP (typically Labour and the Scottish National Party in Scotland) have their list votes adjusted *downwards*.
- The overall effect of variable top-up is to make the total result nearly proportional to the total votes cast in both systems.

Single Transferable Vote (STV)

STV is the system used for all elections in Northern Ireland. It is also used for local government elections in Scotland and for general elections in the Republic of Ireland. It is commonly described as a proportional system.

It is a complex system, especially when it comes to counting and the establishment of the result. This is how it works. Some detail has been omitted, but the following details are what you need to know:

- There are six seats available in each constituency.
- Each party is permitted to put up as many candidates as there are seats, i.e. up to six. In practice, parties do not adopt six candidates as they have no chance of winning all six seats available. Four is the normal maximum number from each party.
- Voters place the candidates in their order of preference by placing a number 1, 2, 3, etc. beside their names.
- Voters can vote for candidates from different parties or even all the parties, though few actually do.

- At the count an **electoral quota** is calculated. This is established by taking the total number of votes cast, and dividing it by the number of seats available plus 1. So, if 50,000 votes were cast and six seats are available, the quota is $50{,}000 \div (6+1=7)$. This works out as 7,142. One is then added, giving a final figure of 7,143.
- At first all the first preferences are counted for each candidate. Any candidates who achieve the quota are elected automatically.
- After this stage the counting is complex. Essentially the second and subsequent preferences from the ballot papers of the elected candidates are added to the other candidates. If this results in an individual achieving the quota, he or she is elected.
- This process continues until six candidates have achieved the quota and are elected.

The complex counting system is designed to ensure that voters' preferences are aggregated to ensure that the six most popular candidates *overall* will be elected. The overall outcome tends to be highly proportional, with each party achieving its fair share of seats (see Table 7.4 below).

The 2016 devolved elections and their outcomes

Scotland

Table 7.1 shows the effects of the Additional Member System (AMS) very clearly, especially if we look at columns (3) and (6), headed '% of list votes won' and '% of total seats won'. This tells us how proportional the system is in terms of its outcome. How close are these two numbers? The answer is quite close. The Scottish National Party (SNP), for example, won 41.7% of the votes cast in the regional list system — a good test of popular support for the party — and it won 48.8% of the total seats available. So it did gain a 'winner's bonus', but not a decisive one. The other four parties gained a proportion of the seats approximately in line with their popularity at the poll. The two smallest parties were slightly disadvantaged (their disadvantage was transferred to the winning SNP) but, again, this was not decisive.

Table 7.1 The Scottish Parliament (showing only parties which won seats)

(1) Party	(2) Constituency seats won	(3) % of list votes won	(4) List seats awarded (top-up)	(5) Total seats won	(6) % of total seats won
SNP	59	41.7	4	63	48.8
Conservative	7	22.9	24	31	24.0
Labour	3	19.1	21	24	18.6
Green	0	6.6	6	6	4.7
Lib Dem	4	5.2	1	5	3.9
Totals	73		56	129	

Now consider the constituency seats won. Column (1) shows that the SNP won 59 of the 73 seats available in this part of the system. This represents 80.8% of the seats! It would have been a landslide win for the SNP under FPTP, even though its actual popularity stands at just below 50%. Conversely, all the other parties would have been virtually wiped out. However fervent a supporter one is of the Scottish National Party, this would have been an unacceptable result.

We can also see how the differential top-up works. Take the Conservative Party. It won just under 10% (seven out of 73) of the constituencies (column (1), but gained 22.9% (column (3) of the popular votes. As it was heavily disadvantaged by the FPTP part of the system, this was compensated by a bias in the other direction in how many 'list' seats it was awarded. Column (4) shows that the party was awarded 24 out of the 56 top-up seats available. The Green Party actually won no seats at all under FPTP but was awarded six top-up seats as it gained 6.6% of the popular vote and this needed to be recognised. Interestingly, the Liberal Democrats won four constituencies but ended up with fewer overall seats than the Greens. This was fair as the Greens won a higher proportion of the popular vote (6.6% against 5.2%).

We can now summarise the impact of using AMS as opposed to FPTP in Scotland:
- It prevented any party winning an overall majority. Under FPTP the SNP would have won an undesirable landslide.
- The Conservatives and the Labour Party won their fair share of the seats. This meant that there could be effective parliamentary opposition, which would have been missing under FPTP.
- Small parties did gain some deserved representation.

In terms of government formation, the electoral system also did its job well. The SNP could and did form a government as a single party because it controlled almost half the seats in parliament. However, it was still a minority government and so would need regularly to secure the agreement of at least one of the other parties to any legislative proposals; it was a compromise between strong, decisive government and government which is accountable and can be controlled by parliament if necessary.

Wales

The characteristics of the outcome in the Welsh Assembly election were remarkably similar to what happened in Scotland. Here again there was a dominant party but it could not quite win an overall majority. Here, though, Labour won an even bigger winner's bonus than the SNP in Scotland. UKIP was the biggest winner in the impact of AMS. The party failed to win a single constituency but was awarded seven top-up seats and so gained a meaningful toe-hold in the assembly. Labour formed a minority government.

Table 7.2 The Welsh Assembly (showing only parties which won seats)

Party	Constituency seats won	% of list votes won	List seats awarded (top-up)	Total seats won	% of total seats won
Labour	27	31.5	2	29	48.3
Plaid Cymru	6	20.8	6	12	20.0
Conservative	6	18.8	5	11	18.3
UKIP	0	13.0	7	7	11.7
Lib Dem	1	6.5	0	1	1.7
Totals	40		20	60	

London

The effects of AMS were especially important in the London Assembly election. The election of the new mayor took place on the same day. Sadiq Khan, the Labour candidate, was the winner. A key role of the assembly is to call the mayor to account. Had Labour won a majority in the assembly, such accountability would have been considerably weakened. Almost as importantly, it would have been *seen* to be weak. Labour won nine of the 14 constituencies in London but just failed to win an overall majority when the top-up seats were added. So the mayor can be brought to account more effectively. It was also important that small parties won some representation in London.

Table 7.3 The London Assembly (showing only parties which won seats)

Party	Constituency seats won	% of list votes won	List seats awarded	Total seats won	% of total seats won
Labour	9	40.3	3	12	48.0
Conservative	5	29.2	3	8	32.0
Green	0	8.0	2	2	8.0
UKIP	0	6.5	2	2	8.0
Lib Dem	0	6.3	1	1	4.0
Totals	14			25	

Northern Ireland

Under a different system, single transferable vote (STV), the outcome of the Northern Ireland Assembly looked rather different from the outcomes of the AMS elections elsewhere. However, Northern Ireland did share one common feature with the others — the proportion of seats won by each party *was* reasonably close to the proportion of *first preference* votes cast for those parties (see Table 7.4). Once again, too, the biggest party, the Democratic Unionists, gained a small 'bonus', but also not decisively.

Table 7.4 The Northern Ireland Assembly (showing only parties which won seats)

Party	% first preference votes	Seats won	% seats won
Democratic Unionist	29.2	38	35.2
Sinn Fein	24.0	28	25.9
Ulster Unionist	12.6	16	14.8
Social Democratic and Labour (SDLP)	12.0	12	11.1
Alliance	7.0	8	7.4
Green	2.7	2	1.9
People Before Profit	2.0	2	1.9
Traditional Unionist Voice (TUV)	3.4	1	0.9
Independent	3.3	1	0.9
Total		108	

There is no single dominant party in Northern Ireland. In contrast, five parties won significant representation, three others won some seats and one independent candidate was elected. All things seem possible under STV. This is because candidates can benefit from second, third and subsequent preference votes. If every seat were awarded on *first and only* preferences (as they are with FPTP), only three parties would win any significant representation. This is especially important in Northern Ireland.

The province is a very divided society. There are two distinct communities, the largely Protestant British loyalists and the Catholic Irish nationalists. These two groups are also divided between moderates and extremists, making four sections. Add those who do not feel themselves politically motivated by religion or nationalism (represented largely by the Alliance Party) and the division of the political system into five parties becomes explicable. This multi-party system was essential in creating a power-sharing system of government where no community could feel dominant and no community would feel oppressed.

Conclusion

Electoral systems do not exist in a vacuum; they are part of the political system and, to some extent, they shape it. If, therefore, we ask the question 'Does the electoral system reflect the political structure of society accurately and does it produce effective and representative government?', the evidence of the 2016 devolved elections is that both AMS and STV are successful. PR, either in its hybrid AMS form, or in its pure form of STV, does work.

Chapter 8

Elected mayors: a new start for local democracy?

Exam success

The up-to-date facts, examples and arguments in this chapter will help you to produce good-quality answers in your AS unit tests in the following areas of the specifications.

Edexcel	AQA	OCR
Unit 1	**Unit 2**	**Unit F852**
Democracy and political participation	Multi-level governance	Constitution
Unit 2		
Constitution		

A word of caution

Before examining the issue of elected mayors it is important particularly, for those who are not familiar with local government arrangements in the UK, to understand the distinction between *elected* mayors and *honorary* mayors. Local councils representing towns and cities have for centuries chosen a mayor — often also known as 'Lord Mayor' — as an honour given to a prominent citizen, usually a long-serving member of the elected council. These honorary mayors are little more than figureheads. They carry out ceremonial duties at important local occasions and meet visiting dignitaries, but have no special political role. They also normally hold office for only one year. The Lord Mayor of London — usually an important figure in the financial world — is the best known of such mayors. In fact he or she only represents the *City* of London, the so-called 'square mile' that contains the headquarters of many financial institutions. The folk-tale hero Dick Whittington was such a mayor. We are not concerned here with these honorary mayors.

Elected mayors were first seen in 2000 in London and it is these mayors that concern us here. It should also be said that this chapter applies only to England and Wales. Scotland (where a mayor is known as a provost) and Northern Ireland now make their own arrangements for local governance.

Context

In 1999 Parliament passed the **Greater London Authority Act**, setting up the office of an elected mayor for Greater London, backed by an elected assembly of 25 members. The mayor is elected by the Supplementary Vote (SV) method and the London Assembly through the Additional Member System (AMS). Since then the elected mayors of London have been:

- 2000   Ken Livingstone   Labour
- 2004   Ken Livingstone   Labour
- 2008   Boris Johnson   Conservative
- 2012   Boris Johnson   Conservative
- 2016   Sadiq Khan   Labour

After the office of London mayor was established, the issue of elected mayors moved to the bottom of the political agenda. London was seen as a special case, as there was then no strategic authority for the city. Cities elsewhere in England were already governed by elected councils. Each council had a leader, normally the head of the majority party or coalition on the council. No such arrangement had existed in London since 1986 when the Greater London Council was abolished. The elected mayor filled the gap.

The **Local Government Act, 2000** allowed local authorities (not just cities, but also localities and boroughs) to introduce an elected mayor, backed by a cabinet made up of elected councillors. It was not an especially popular idea. Only 13 localities introduced elected mayors as a result of the legislation. These included Hartlepool in the northeast, where Stuart Drummond, the local football team's mascot, ran as a novelty independent candidate and, to everybody's surprise, won; Middlesbrough; Torbay in Devon; and Tower Hamlets, an east London borough.

The coalition government, elected in 2010, resurrected the idea of elected mayors, largely as a result of Liberal Democrat demands. The **Localism Act, 2011** allowed for cities to hold referendums on whether to adopt an elected mayor. By the time the Act came into force, two cities — Leicester and Liverpool — had already decided to adopt elected mayors. Ten cities held referendums on the issue in 2012, but only one — Bristol — voted to hold elections. Once again the policy seemed to be foundering on the rocks of local apathy and opposition.

Undaunted, the coalition government announced new devolution proposals. These involved the negotiation of so-called devolution deals (see below), whereby new local authorities would have increased powers and more financial independence but, in return, would have to establish an elected mayor.

Table 8.1 summarises the main legislation concerning elected mayors.

Table 8.1 Legislation concerning elected mayors

Act	Main provisions
Greater London Authority Act, 1999	Introduced an elected mayor for Greater London. It also established a London Assembly, which was to hold the mayor to account.
Local Government Act, 2000	Gave cities the option of introducing an elected mayor, backed by a cabinet of local councillors.
Localism Act, 2011	Allowed cities to hold referendums to determine whether the local population wanted an elected mayor.
Cities and Local Government Devolution Act, 2016	Confirmed the provision of devolution deals (see below), many of which had already been negotiated. Some local authorities were allowed to come together to form a region and create an elected mayoralty. In new regions and existing cities, devolution deals were to be arranged with central government.

The devolution deals

From 2014 onwards the coalition pressed ahead with plans for more devolution of powers and more elected mayors. The new policy involved introducing incentives for local cities and regions to introduce elected mayors. The incentives were the transfer of greater powers together with more financial independence. The policy has five main objectives:

1 **To devolve wide powers to English cities and regions.** These powers include transport, planning, economic development, housing and policing. It is possible that more powers will be devolved in future.

2 **To grant greater financial independence to such authorities.** This mainly involves the ability of local authorities to retain the business rates they collect (business rates are local taxes on commercial premises). Large authorities will also be allowed to borrow money from financial markets for large-scale capital projects, to be paid for from additional business rates.

3 **To introduce elected mayors wherever such devolution deals are concluded.** This also includes redrawing local government boundaries. Cities such as Liverpool, Sheffield and Manchester are to be turned into larger 'city regions', ranging in size from about 1 million people to over 2 million. In addition, some non-city regions will be created. Table 8.2 shows some examples of the new authorities. Elections for mayors will be held during 2017.

4 **By so doing, to improve the state of local democracy and accountability.** The extent to which this may be achieved is considered below.

5 **To help spread economic activity more widely, away from London and the southeast.** The policy is connected with the HS2 project to build a high-speed

rail link to the Midlands and north of England, plus the creation of a 'Northern Hub' based in Manchester where large-scale capital investment will take place. This is sometimes described as 'rebalancing the UK economy'.

Each 'deal' with each new authority is different and the terms will vary. Clearly it is the city regions which will enjoy the widest powers and the greatest autonomy.

Table 8.2 Examples of new city regions and combined authorities, 2017

New authority	Population
West Midlands Combined Authority	2.8 million
Manchester City Region	2.7 million
East Anglia Combined Authority	2.4 million
Sheffield City Region	1.8 million
Liverpool City Region	1.5 million
West of England Combined Authority	1.1 million

It should be noted, however, that some of these deals are still being disputed, especially in combined authorities, and it may be that elections scheduled for 2017 will be cancelled.

How might the policy enhance democracy?

There are a number of important considerations here. Supporters claim the following benefits:

- Local government suffers from chronic voter apathy. Turnouts at local elections are notoriously low, usually falling between 20 and 40%. By devolving more powers and introducing an elected figurehead, it is hoped to revitalise local interest.
- The plans to devolve considerable powers away from London to cities and regions are expected to lead to better accountability and renewed involvement by the public. One of the principal outcomes of devolution in general is said to be that, by bringing government closer to the people, there is better democratic control.
- The concentration of power into a single figure — the mayor — may well improve the 'strategic' government of these regions. It will be possible to develop a long-term plan for the development of cities and regions in accordance with public wishes. By rationalising local government and bringing disparate authorities together, it is hoped that local government will be better understood, and that this better understanding will enhance local democracy.
- Accountability will be improved. As well as electing a mayor, the voters will be able to 'un-elect' him or her. He or she will become the key figure in terms of political responsibility. As things stand, local elections tend to be won and lost on *national* issues — how popular the national government is or is not, for example — while the new arrangement may bring local issues to the fore.

- If the experience of London is replicated, the new elected posts may attract high-profile figures who will become well known in the locality, very much along the lines of London, New York and Paris in the past. Again, this may create renewed interest in local politics. Table 8.3 shows some of the more interesting contenders.

Table 8.3 Potential and actual contenders for election as mayor in 2017

Contender	Party	Background	City or region
Andy Street	Conservative	Managing director of John Lewis Partnership	West Midlands
Andy Burnham	Labour	Former health secretary and cabinet minister	Manchester
Steve Rotherham	Labour	A very popular local MP and close associate of Jeremy Corbyn	Liverpool
Sion Simon	Labour	A former junior minister under Gordon Brown	West Midlands

What are the potential problems?

The policy of introducing elected mayors may well not be as successful as many hope. Among the dangers are these:

- Apathy. In the most recent London mayoral election in 2016, the turnout was only 42.3%. If the London turnout is that low, it is likely to be even lower in other areas which have lower levels of political engagement. Low turnouts will severely damage accountability.
- If it is perceived that mayors have fewer powers than was first thought (central government is notoriously reluctant to give up any of its powers), people may become disillusioned. In addition, the position of mayor may attract low-calibre candidates.
- Most *city* mayors will inevitably be Labour Party members. Support for Labour is much stronger in urban areas. When there is a Conservative government, this may lead to constant political deadlock. Ken Livingstone (Labour) and Boris Johnson (Conservative) were London mayor when, for all or most of their time, the central government was of the same party as themselves. This will not always be the case as the new London mayor, Sadiq Khan, is about to discover.
- It is claimed that elected mayors and everything that goes with them will prove to be expensive. In particular, local businesses may end up paying additional taxes for the activities of the new mayors.

Conclusion

There are still many battles to be fought over the introduction of elected mayors. Some localities are resisting their introduction. It may well be that the idea will only be effectively introduced in the city regions, where mayors are to be known as 'metro-mayors'.

The question of whether this represents a new start for local democracy will probably depend upon two conditions. First, how will local populations react to the changes? Will they embrace or reject the concept of a mayor? Will they follow London in embracing the concept or will they largely ignore it? Second, how will central government deal with the change? There are already signs that the new prime minister, Theresa May, is less enthusiastic about city devolution than its main sponsor, George Osborne. Indeed, Osborne was dismissed by Mrs May as one of her first acts of government.

The early signs are not good. Many local authorities resisted the introduction of elected mayors and it is likely that there will be many fewer successful transfers to the new system than government had originally hoped for. If mayors do not receive additional powers and financial independence in the future, they may well become little more than figureheads, elected by small numbers of voters. This has been the fate of elected police commissioners, who have few powers and attract very little interest from voters.

If elected mayors are to become a significant factor in local and regional government, it is essential that communities turn out to vote in large numbers for candidates, and that central government is serious about decentralising power.

Exam focus

To consolidate your knowledge of this chapter, answer the following questions:

1 How can elected mayors enhance democracy?
2 What are the main objectives of city devolution?
3 Why are turnouts at local elections invariably very low?
4 What problems may arise as a result of the introduction of elected mayors in England and Wales?

Chapter 9

The Liberal Democrats: do they have a future?

Exam success

The up-to-date facts, examples and arguments in this chapter will help you to produce good-quality answers in your AS unit tests in the following areas of the specifications.

Edexcel	AQA	OCR
Unit 1	**Unit 1**	**Unit F851**
Party policies and ideas	Political parties	Political parties

Context

The Liberal Democrat Party suffered a massive defeat in the 2015 general election. The party's representation in the House of Commons plummeted from 57 to just 8 and its share of the vote fell from 23.0% to 7.9%. The party lost all 15 of its seats in the southwest of England, a traditional stronghold, and was soundly beaten in London.

It was generally agreed that the main reason for this defeat went back to a broken promise by the party leader, Nick Clegg, not to support a rise in university tuition fees. After that, several other factors were at work, including:

- As the junior partner in the coalition, the party, and its leader in particular, were seen as weak alongside the dominant Conservatives.
- The weakness of the party was exemplified by a number of policy failures, such as ineffective opposition to severe cuts in welfare benefits, a poor campaign to reform the electoral system and the inability to force through reform of the House of Lords.
- While the Conservatives accepted the credit for the improving economic situation, the Liberal Democrats took the blame for austerity and welfare cuts.
- Liberal Democrat policy successes, such as raising the starting level for paying income tax, helping low-income families, preventing the worst examples of benefit cuts and the introduction of more free nursery places, tended to be ignored by the electorate, possibly because the party failed to present itself in a positive enough light.

After the election, Nick Clegg resigned as leader and the relatively unknown Tim Farron took over. The party also lost several of its most experienced politicians — some of them former ministers in the coalition — such as Vince Cable (business secretary) and Danny Alexander (treasury chief secretary, effectively deputy chancellor of the exchequer).

In the local government elections in spring 2016, the Liberal Democrats did gain a small number of seats — 45 — but this was modest in a field where Liberal Democrats traditionally do well. In the 2016 elections to the Scottish Parliament and Welsh Assembly, the party also performed relatively poorly in terms of votes and seats won.

In the light of all these negative indications, together with the fluidity of party politics currently in the UK, this chapter seeks to address the question of whether the Liberal Democrats have a future.

The centre-left in the UK

The Liberal Democrats can be described a centre-left party. By this, we mean the party has the following key characteristics:

- The dominance of free-market capitalism is accepted, but there is a need for the state to regulate capitalism, protecting both consumers and workers, though stopping short of public ownership (nationalisation) of private enterprise.
- There is an emphasis on the protection of rights for both individuals and various groups in society. The centre-left generally champions minority rights.
- Equality for individuals and sections of society is to be promoted and protected.
- While centre-left politicians accept the inevitability of economic inequality within free-market capitalism, they seek to reduce poverty and to close the gap between the rich and the poor through taxation and welfare.
- There is strong support for a state-led and run welfare state.
- A stress is laid on equality of opportunity, especially through the provision of good education for all.
- Protection for workers through legal safeguards is essential. Trade union rights are to be protected but unions are not to be given any special status.

There may be considerable variation among centre-left politicians over such issues as energy policy, foreign affairs, defence and constitutional reform, but the list above represents their typical core values.

The centre-left in the UK is a crowded field. Seven parties occupy the political ground. This compares with the centre-right, which is dominated by the Conservatives and contains only four significant parties. Table 9.1 shows the number of votes won by the various centre-left and centre-right parties in the UK in the 2015 general election.

Table 9.1 Voting for the centre-left and centre-right, 2015 general election

Party	Votes won	% of total votes
The centre-left		
Labour	9,347,324	30.4
Liberal Democrat	2,415,862	7.9
Scottish National Party	1,454,436	4.7

Table 9.1 Voting for the centre-left and centre-right, 2015 general election (Continued)

The centre-left		
Green Party	1,157,613	3.8
Plaid Cymru (Wales)	181,704	0.6
Sinn Fein (Northern Ireland)	176,232	0.6
SDLP (Northern Ireland)	99,809	0.3
Total centre-left voting	14,832,980	48.3
The centre-right		
Conservative	11,300,109	36.8
UKIP	3,881,099	12.6
DUP (Northern Ireland)	184,260	0.6
UUP (Northern Ireland)	114,935	0.4
Total centre-right voting	15,480,403	50.4
Others	378,297	1.3

We can see from Table 9.1 that there is a close balance between the centre-left and centre-right in terms of voter popularity. However, given that UKIP took votes fairly evenly from Labour and the Conservatives, if it proves unable to maintain its impact after the EU referendum and having lost its charismatic leader, Nigel Farage, the centre-left might gain a slight advantage as a result of UKIP's potential decline.

The problem for this grouping remains, however, that the left in UK politics is highly fragmented, especially if we consider the widening split in the Labour Party, whereas the right is more consolidated around the Conservative Party. This means, as students of the electoral system will know, that the right is almost always bound to win elections under the first-past-the-post system (FPTP). This creates another difficulty for the Liberal Democrats, one which they have faced for many years.

Green shoots

The question is: are there any signs of a Liberal Democrat recovery? The answer is: yes, there are, but they remain very modest. These signs include:

- Since the 2015 election the party has attracted a substantial number of new members. Around 15,000 new members signed up after the EU referendum. However, a word of caution is needed here, as this was a response to leader Tim Farron's assertion that the party would fight to get the UK back into the EU — something that is unlikely to be achieved.
- The Liberal Democrats won some seats in the local government elections in England in 2016 and gained two constituency seats in the 2016 Scottish parliamentary elections.

- In September 2016 the Liberal Democrats made five gains in local council by-elections, winning seats from Labour, the Conservatives and UKIP. They also held on to some potentially vulnerable seats.
- The Liberal Democrats did exceptionally well in a by-election, in October 2016, for David Cameron's former seat in Witney. The party beat Labour into second place and slashed the Conservative majority from over 25,000 in 2015 to just below 6,000.

Naturally, the Liberal Democrats leadership has drawn some comfort from these developments but perhaps the phrase 'clutching at straws' is more appropriate than 'green shoots'.

There are a few possible ways forward for the Liberal Democrats, even if they do not increase their vote significantly. Among them are:
- **Electoral pacts.** An electoral pact between two or more parties is an agreement whereby they agree that, in some constituencies where either but not both parties has a chance to win, one of the two parties will not put up a candidate and will tell its supporters to vote for the other party in the agreement. Labour and the Green Party would be potential partners in such a pact.
- **Rainbow coalitions.** If the Conservative Party is unable to win an overall majority in a future election, the Liberal Democrats could be part of a wider coalition of several centre-left parties to form a majority. Such coalitions are common in the rest of Europe.
- **Amalgamations.** It is possible that the Liberal Democrats will be courted by another party with a view to coming together to form a bigger party. This is how the Liberal Democrats came into existence in 1988 when the Liberal Party and the Social Democrat Party joined forces. This is most likely to occur if the Labour Party splits into two and the moderate wing considers joining the Liberal Democrats.

Negative indications

Despite the modest positive signs, the Liberal Democrats still face a huge uphill struggle to recover their position. The problems they face include these:
- Though they have increased their membership, so have other parties, notably Labour, the Scottish Nationalists and the Green Party. The new members may reflect an increased post-Brexit interest in politics *in general* rather than a growth in the particular attractions of the Liberal Democrats.
- The opinion polls still show only about 8% of voters saying they would vote for the Liberal Democrats — in other words, no change from 2015.
- The proposed new electoral boundaries and reduction in the size of the House of Commons from 650 to 600 will adversely affect the Liberal Democrats, who may lose up to half of their already meagre representation in parliament, including Nick Clegg's Sheffield seat.

Table 9.2 presents the result of an opinion poll by Ipsos Mori taken in August 2016. It shows that Tim Farron's persistent negative net approval rating will not go away. The only consolation for Farron is that he is not in as poor a position as Jeremy Corbyn!

Table 9.2 Approval ratings of three party leaders, August 2016

Leader	Positive rating (%)	Negative rating (%)
Theresa May	54	19
Jeremy Corbyn	26	55
Tim Farron	22	30

Source: Ipsos Mori

Conclusion

The Liberal Democrat Party is at a low ebb. It could be argued that it is at its lowest point since its formation in 1988. Its short-term prospects remain bleak according to most of the evidence. However, if we consider the long-term position, the party has some hope. There are a number of reasons for this:

- The party has retained a strong, active membership and remains well organised at local level.
- It also retains a large, powerful presence in the House of Lords, with 101 peers taking the Liberal Democrat whip in October 2016.
- It has a long and celebrated tradition which means that voters may well return to the party in the future.
- It is a united party, in direct contrast to Labour.
- The possible demise of the Labour Party may provide an opportunity for the Liberal Democrats to fill a gap in the centre-left of politics, at least in England and Wales.
- In the long term, the party may be able to distance itself from the mistakes it made in the coalition period from 2010 to 2015.

All is not yet lost for the Liberal Democrats, but the party's future prospects remain very uncertain.

Exam focus

To consolidate your knowledge of this chapter, answer the following questions:

1 What is meant by the term 'centre-left'?
2 Why are small parties at a disadvantage in UK politics?
3 Why did the Liberal Democrats lose so many seats in the 2015 general election?
4 What is a rainbow coalition and how might it arise?
5 What are electoral pacts? How and why might they work?

Chapter 10

Public opinion polls: time for regulation?

Context

Public opinion polls have been a feature of British political life since the 1940s when the first poll by the Gallup organisation (an American company that had started polling in the USA before the Second World War) predicted that Labour would win the 1945 general election, much to the surprise of most commentators of the day. Gallup was right and from then on polls became increasingly used to gauge political opinion.

There were no problems with the polls for many years. They were reasonably accurate and did not seem to have any impact on the way people voted or how campaigning politicians behaved. They were used mostly by newspapers to inform and entertain their readers. In 2010, however, attention was drawn to the polls during the UK general election campaign of that year. What was different about 2010?

In the weeks leading up to that election, the polls were all predicting that neither of the main parties would win an overall majority. It was, in short, going to be a 'hung parliament'. Suddenly the political landscape changed. The main reason for this was a prediction that the Liberal Democrats were surging in popularity following a strong performance by their leader, Nick Clegg. Indeed, just three weeks before the election date the polls showed them ahead of Labour and just behind the Conservatives on 30% of the predicted popular vote. It is generally agreed that this caused a falling off in support for the Liberal Democrats, as many people feared that there would be a weak coalition or an even weaker minority government. Liberal Democrat support declined and the party only won 23.6% of the vote in the actual election in May, well below the prediction in the earlier polls.

For the first time, it seemed that the polls' predictions may have been significantly influencing voting behaviour. In the event there was a hung parliament and a coalition ensued, but the first serious question marks were appearing over the role of polling. Then in the 2015 general election a new problem arose. The polls began to get it wrong. Their predictions became far removed from the actual voting outcome. When this happened again in the 2016 referendum on EU membership, a clamour grew for some kind of regulation of the polls.

The Scottish independence referendum, 2014

For most of the run-up to the vote on Scottish independence, the opinion polls were predicting a comfortable victory for the 'No to Independence' side. Then, with a few weeks to go, two polls showed a different result. These were produced by YouGov and ICM, two of the most prominent and respected polling organisations. They both showed 'Yes to Independence' ahead. This might not have been a significant development, had it not been for the fact that the results sent shockwaves through Westminster. Suddenly there was a real possibility that Scotland might vote for independence.

This resulted in all the main parties meeting together to devise a plan designed to ward off independence. The strategy was to grant Scotland considerable additional devolved powers, including control over income tax and over welfare payments — a huge shift in the distribution of power. It was hoped that this promise would reduce the Scots' enthusiasm for full independence. Two opinion polls had caused a dramatic change in the UK's constitutional arrangements.

The plan worked. Later polls showed a movement back towards 'No' and, in the referendum itself, the Scots voted 55–45% to remain in the United Kingdom. Table 10.1 shows the change in the two polls in question.

Table 10.1 Two key polls and Scottish independence

Polling organisation	Date	%* yes to independence	%* no to independence
ICM	10–11 Sept	49	42
YouGov	2–5 Sept	47	45
ICM	12–16 Sept	41	45
YouGov	15–17 Sept	45	49
Result	**18 Sept**	**45**	**55**

*rounded to nearest whole number

We can see from Table 10.1 that the earlier polls showed leads for 'Yes', but that the position was reversed a few days later. The explanation is probably that, between the two polls, the promises offered by Westminster politicians to transfer considerable new powers to the Scottish government had worked.

As a postscript to this analysis, we can see that the polls underestimated the vote for 'No'. This was true of most of the opinion polls, which averaged about 45% for 'Yes' — the final result — but only about 50% for 'No' — the result was 55%. This suggests that there had been a late swing towards 'No' or perhaps that most of the undecided voters opted for the status quo at the last minute. Opinion polls struggle to predict such late swings, as it takes several days to process results.

The 2015 general election

The first question arising from 2015 is not specifically about polling accuracy or inaccuracy; it concerns the influence of Scotland. The polls consistently suggested a hung parliament, with the Scottish National Party forecast to win most of the seats in Scotland and so end up holding the balance of power in the UK House of Commons. Conservatives played on this fear, suggesting that Scottish first minister, Nicola Sturgeon, would end up calling the shots on a weak, minority Labour government. This may explain why there was a late swing towards the Conservatives. Had the polls been accurate and predicted a Conservative majority, this fear may not have influenced voters so much.

Table 10.2 shows what the polls were predicting, in terms of the overall popular vote, in the few days before the general election, which took place on 7 May. At the bottom of the table we show the actual result.

Table 10.2 Final opinion polls before the 2015 general election

Polling organisation	Date	Con (%)*	Lab (%)*	Lib Dem (%)*	UKIP (%)*	Green (%)*
Populus	7 May	33	33	10	14	5
ICM	7 May	34	35	9	11	4
Panelbase	6 May	31	33	8	16	5
YouGov	6 May	34	34	10	12	4
Ashcroft	6 May	33	33	10	11	6
IpsosMori	6 May	36	35	8	11	5
Survation	5 May	33	34	9	16	4
ComRes	5 May	35	32	9	14	4
Result	**7 May**	**37**	**30**	**8**	**13**	**4**

* rounded to nearest whole number
Source: BBC

The figures are striking. There was remarkable consistency between the polls. If they were wrong, they were all wrong in the same direction. They all showed a virtual dead heat between the two main parties. These statistics were converted into a prediction that no party would win an overall majority. There would be another hung parliament, the polls were asserting.

But, most importantly, the polls were simply wrong. All of them under-estimated the Conservative vote and over-estimated Labour support. Later research suggested there had *not* been a late swing to the Conservatives which could not have been reflected in the polls. So the main question is: what *did* go wrong? A secondary question is: did the opinion polls influence voting? Specifically, did some voters, fearing another coalition, switch to the Conservatives when they saw the poll predictions of a close finish? As we saw above, did they avoid a hung parliament to keep the Scots out of power?

The British Polling Council inquiry

There was so much concern over the poor performance of the opinion polls in 2015 that an inquiry was undertaken by the British Polling Council in 2015–16 to see what had gone wrong. The council rejected a number of theories about why the polls might have been wrong. The rejected explanations included the following:

- There was a very late swing to the Conservatives.
- Some Conservatives, reluctant to admit they were Tories, misreported their voting intentions to the pollsters. These voters, known as 'shy Tories', were not a significant factor.
- There are 'lazy' Labour supporters — that is, Labour supporters who intend to support the party, but then don't bother to vote on the day. Again, these were not seen as a significant group.
- The increase in postal voting might have skewed the outcome, as postal voting intention would not appear in the later polls. This was rejected, as postal voting seems to have shown a very similar pattern to conventional voting.
- The polling organisations might have processed the data inaccurately. The fact that all the polls were wrong in the same way suggested this could not be true. They could not all have made the same mistakes.

The British Polling Council inquiry did come to one firm conclusion — that the errors were caused by the way in which virtually all the pollsters select their samples. They nearly all use what is called the **quota method**, while the British Polling Council recommends **random sampling**. Random sampling is considered by most researchers to be more accurate than the quota method. However, the quota method is less expensive. Briefly the difference between the two methods is this:

- The **quota method** involves constructing a specific sample that is proportionately representative of voters overall — for example, it will be half female, contain about 10% members of ethnic minorities, will be from different parts of the country and will have a representative age profile. Polling organisations mostly use between 1,000 and 2,000-person samples.
- The **random sample** is what it sounds. It is a completely random selection of people. As long as it is large enough (which is the problem), it is statistically likely to be representative of the whole population. Furthermore, there is no bias in selecting the subjects who answer the question. The larger size of such samples raises the cost.

The inquiry concluded that there were faults in the way polling companies were constructing their quotas and that the errors always seemed to produce polling results which indicated more people likely to vote Labour than existed in the whole population. It accepted that the pollsters were unlikely to switch to random samples, but said that they should address the quota problem.

The Regulation of Political Opinion Polling Bill, 2015–16

This was a private members' bill sponsored by Lord Foulkes and Christopher Chope MP. It did not become law as it lacked government support, but it may influence the government to consider such a measure in the future. Its main terms (and therefore recommendations) were these:

- It would establish a Political Opinion Polling Regulation Authority.
- Such an authority would regulate the way samples are constructed.
- It would also regulate the way in which questioning is undertaken.
- It would consider whether polling should be suspended for a given period before a referendum or election.

The British Polling Council opposed the measure and got its way. Its president, John Curtice, is possibly Britain's most celebrated psephologist (expert on elections and voting behaviour). His comments, opposing regulation, are given in Box 10.1.

> ### Box 10.1   Curtice on poll regulation
>
> What is needed now is a critical and open appraisal of where the polls went wrong, not the heavy hand of regulation that in attempting to impose common standards would make it more likely that the polls all get it wrong again in future. As any economic forecaster knows too well, forecasting how people will behave is always a difficult enterprise. No-one has yet suggested that, despite their many errors, economic forecasting should be regulated, and it is not clear why attempting to anticipate how people will vote should be treated any differently.
>
> Source: British Polling Council

The Council argued that the problems could be solved if sampling methods were improved. The main reasons for opposing a ban on publishing polls in the run-up to a vote was that they would be published abroad anyway and would become private, only available to wealthy organisations.

The EU referendum, 2016

Just when it seemed that things could not get worse for opinion polling, they did. Along came the EU referendum. Naturally, there was huge interest in how opinion was moving in the run-up to this epoch-making event. But, as in 2015, the polls got it wrong. Table 10.3 shows the predictions of the main polls in the last few days before the referendum, and the final result.

Table 10.3 Final opinion polls before the EU referendum

Polling organisation	Phone or online?	Date	% remain	% leave
Ipsos Mori	Phone	14 June	49	43
Survation	Phone	20 June	45	44
YouGov	Online	22 June	45	45
Com Res	Phone	22 June	48	42
TNS	Online	22 June	41	43
Opinium	Online	22 June	44	45
Result		**24 June**	**48***	**52***

* actual voting numbers are higher because 'don't knows' are not shown in the polling statistics

Source: BBC

Most of the polls were wrong in predicting that the UK would vote to remain in the European Union. It is feared, mostly by EU supporters, it has to be said, that the predictions of a 'Remain' win may have led to some complacency. However, there is another clue in these data. It is clear that the polls conducted online were more accurate than those conducted by phone. There is a theory that some respondents may lie to researchers when speaking to them, but are more likely to tell the truth online. It may be that some potential voters were too ashamed to admit to another person that they were voting 'Leave', for fear of being branded a racist.

As yet there is no research available on why the polls were wrong. There might have been a very late swing towards 'Leave', though many undecided voters tend to vote for the status quo. Whatever the reason, it was another blow to the polling industry.

Conclusion

It now seems unlikely that there will be any regulation of political opinion polls. However, it may well be that, as the polls fall into disrepute, they will gradually decline in use. This is a potentially dangerous situation if they are replaced by speculation in the news media or, more seriously, the social media. It seems preferable to rely on scientific evidence, even if it is not fully accurate.

The best hope for the polls is that they improve their sampling methods and possibly switch to random sampling. Online polling seems more accurate than telephone research, although online research does eliminate the small minority of people, mostly elderly, who are not online (just as telephone polling eliminates those people, mostly young, who no longer use a landline). Most likely, though, is that the publication of poll results will be banned in the run-up to an election or referendum.

Italy (for 15 days) and France (for 7 days) ban publication of polls in the days before a vote to reduce the possibility that they may influence voters. Table 10.4 summarises the arguments for and against such a plan.

Table 10.4 Arguments for and against banning opinion polls

For banning them	Against banning them
They may influence the way people vote.	It would infringe the principle of freedom of expression.
They have proved to be inaccurate, so they mislead the public.	If they are banned, they will become available privately for organisations that can afford to pay for them.
Arguably politicians should not be slaves to changing public opinion as expressed in the polls.	Polls give valuable information about people's attitudes which can guide politicians usefully.
	They would still be published abroad and people could access them through the internet.

Finally, there are some reasons why political opinion polls are useful. Assuming that they become more accurate, their advantages include:

- They can inform politicians about the popularity of policies, allowing them to adjust them better to meet the demands of the public.
- Polls can inform undecided voters, helping them make up their minds.
- They provoke political discussion and so promote participation.
- Businesses can plan better for the future if they have some idea about the nature of the future government or the probable outcome of a referendum.

Exam focus

To consolidate your knowledge of this chapter, answer the following questions:

1 How might opinion polls influence the way people vote?
2 Should political opinion polls be banned in the run-up to elections and referendums?
3 To what extent and why are political opinion polls inaccurate?
4 What is the value of political opinion polls?